Getting the Knack

Getting the Knack

20 Poetry Writing Exercises 20

Stephen Dunning

William Stafford

National Council of Teachers of English
1111 Kenyon Road, Urbana, Illinois 61801

NCTE Editorial Board: Keith Gilyard, Ronald Jobe, Joyce Kinkead, Louise W. Phelps, Gladys V. Veidemanis, Charles Suhor, chair, *ex officio*; Michael Spooner, *ex officio*

Manuscript Editor: William Tucker

Production Editor: Rona Smith

Cover Design: Doug Burnett

Interior Design: Doug Burnett

NCTE Stock Number 18488-3050

Library of Congress Cataloging-in-Publication Data

Dunning, Stephen.
    Getting the knack: 20 poetry writing exercises 20/Stephen Dunning, William Stafford.
    p. cm.
    Summary: Introduces different kinds of poems, including headline, letter, recipe, list, and monologue, and provides exercises in writing poems based on both memory and imagination.
    ISBN 0-8141-1848-8
    1. Poetry—Authorship—Juvenile literature. [1. Poetry—Authorship. 2. Creative writing.] I. Stafford, William, 1914- . II. Title.
PN1059.A9D86 1992
808.1—dc20   92-36710
                                         CIP

Contents

Participants

In preparation for this book, many persons wrote poems in response to our trial exercises, and submitted them to us as possible samples. Of the many such gifts received, we selected those few that are printed here. In a more generous world, one with unlimited text space, we'd have included all the work sent to us. But, as it turns out, we had to make choices. How did we do that?

Each of us read all the poems sent us. We each made selections, and once we had those down to a manageable number, we met in Bill's living room and read them again. A long, long session. A few disagreements, many agreements. The names of all the students and teachers who worked with us on this project follow:

Jessica Adkins, Kristen Allison, Cris Anderson, Brooke Harper Bahor, Michael Bailey, Jennifer Barkin, Catherine Barnek, Zach Barnett, Todd Barrow, Sangita Baruah, Deborah Bayer, Michael Behrman, Barbara Bell, Laura Treacy Bentley, Vicki Bergeron, Amy Besel, Erin Bissell, Rob Bixby, Stephanie Block, Janet Bouldin, Brian Bowers, Allison Boye, Amber Brennan, Glynn Bridgewater, Kristy Bronder, Brett Broussard, Laura Brown, Jonathan Bruce, Melissa Burger, William Burns, Janice Byrne, John Callahan, Casey Campbell, Kathy Cardille, Dave Carter, Gabe Ciupek, Andrea Clark, Donna L. Clovis, Bob Coleman, Jean Copland, Bonnie Jean Cousineau, Sarah Cutler, Suzanne Daniels, Christina Darling, Justin Dekker, Derek Dekoff, Ellen Derikart, Lahna Diskin, Michele Donovan, Elizabeth Dorr, Nisha Doshi, Lynne Dozier, Donna Duffy, Danielle A. Durkin, Andrea Duspiva, Christy Eccles, Sharon Eddleston, Louise Eddleston, Ezra Erb, Leslie Byrd Evans, Alyssa Farmer, Pamela B. Farrell, Susan Fasano, Jennifer Ferguson, Margaret Finders;

Priscilla Fletcher, Kathryn Mahoney Fowler, Elizabeth Freimuth, Vanessa Garcia, Tara George, Melissa Glatus, Mike Goettig, Stephen Goff, Kathryn Gonier, Lori LM Goodall, Nicole Gordon, Nancy Gorrell, Suzanne Gorrell, Nancy M. Graham, Kirstin Graslie, Amanda Griffin, Megan Grumbling, Brant Hacker, Deborah Haight, Ron A. Hansen, Stephanie Hare, Sheila R. Hawkins, Cherie Hebert, James Hebert, Randall Heeres, Sally Hellman, Erin Hendel, Kelly Hill, Nona Horsely, Dave Howard, Carol Jago, Lena James, Heather Jennings, Jenny Jernberg, Jennifer Jimenez, Shirley Anna Johnson, Melissa Johnson, Gerry Jones, Robert King, Ann Klein, Christine Kolaya, Dave Korkowski, Amanda LaFond, JoAnn R. Lane, Chad Laporte, Paula

Lee, Michelle Levine, Ly Lim, Courtney Lisgaris, Diane Lockward, Pat Looney, Robert Lortez, Jennifer Main, Danna K. Major, Susie McCoy, Connie McDonald, Bonny McDonald, Nancy McDonald, Anna McEwen, Meredith McGrath, Tracy McMillan, Amanda McNamara, Pamela Merideth, Erin Merz, Mary Moebius, Stephanie Molnar, Sue Moore, Lori Morency, James Mullican, Sheila Murphy;

Shelly Muza, Sivan Nemoricher, Nersi Nikakhtar, Sister Brigid O'Donoghue, Leticia Oberley, Cathy Olmsted, Jennifer Orkis, Michelle Own, Melissa Oxley, Julie Patten, Pepper Phillips, Tracy Phillips, Michelle Pittard, Sharon Plavnick, Jennifer Plunk, Emilynn J. Pumarega, Nalini Raghavan, Sundee Raudabaugh, Regina Reese, Mary Ann Reilly, John Reinhard, Karen Reynolds, Betty Jo Riggs, Jill Roberson, Jackie Robertson, Suzanne Robinson, Jan Robitaille, Holly Rogers, Carey Rollins, Laura Roop, Nancy Allen Rose, Meghan Rosenstein, Jim Rozinsky, April Rudicil, Luanna Russell, Nancy Ryan, Zareh Sarkissian, Kerensa Schendel, Cheryl Schroedter, Charley C. Shaffner, III, Yasmeen Shorish, Abhishek Shrestha, Arielle Siebert, Andrea Siegrist, Ann Marie Skorjanec, George Skornickel, Amber Smith, Regan Smith, April Sorrell, Dori Steavens, Angie Stephenson, Donna-Marie Stupple, Anne McCrary Sullivan, Arlene Swora, Chenoa Taitt, Nicole Tichon, Sadie Tirmizi, Pat Torney, Tracy Valstad, Paule Verdier, Belle Vukovich, Brigitte Wagner-Ott, Amy Waller, Joan Walukonis, Carla Ward, Krista Wark, Michelle Warner, Theresa Waters, Jody Weckerle, Sara Weythman, Misti Williams, Kimberly Williamson, Ashley Wingo, Rachel Woostenholme, Heidi Wortman, Marilyn Yu.

We may have done a good job of choosing, finally. In any case, the responsibility is ours. If you like the poems printed here, smile.

Foreword

Our modest aim for *Getting the Knack* is to help you change your life, for the better.

We mean to speak to those who want to write poems but aren't sure how to start (or how to keep poem-writing going, once it's started). Our exercises tend to be simple. We don't have that much to say to the experienced poet. But for interested beginners we offer do-able work on many kinds of poems; we promise to provide the best examples we can find, and to give specific ways to enter the process of making poems.

Getting the Knack is made up of twenty exercises plus short pieces we call "Interludes"—"written talk" about poetry. Each exercise has action in it. The interludes invite you not to action but to thought. (By the way, you should get a notebook where you can enter your exercise poems and/or your reactions to our interludes.)

How long should you spend on our book? Hard to say. We'd like you to take your time. The effects of some exercises won't sink in right away. So we suggest ten weeks or longer. But if you're in a big hurry, go faster. Whatever your pace, you'll be writing poems, or things-like-poems, very soon.

Now about those pieces you will be writing. They might not interest most others. And might not alter the course of **Literature**. Almost surely you won't load them onto an editor. Not yet.

But your writing might be important, and certainly so for you. You may want to show some pieces around. That's all right. But mostly they'll be practice toward what you'll write once you know how to begin, how to revise, and how to keep up your practice.

Getting the Knack should help you do those things—begin, revise, and practice specific skills. As we said, from the start there will be poems. If you are open to them, your poems may. . .

teach you about yourself

move you toward important feelings and questions

help you probe your memories, feelings, and imagination

make you more optimistic about yourself

and bring more play into your life.

Those are large claims for anything as delicate-looking as a poem! But we believe our claims—that if you pay attention to our exercises and talk, give yourself to them, life will seem even more valuable than it does now.

Ours is a beginning book. A book of beginnings.

It's not likely that *Getting the Knack* will lead you to fortune or fame. But it may encourage you to learn to be a good poet. Some of the persons (young and old) who tested our exercises said that they were going to make room for poetry-writing throughout their lives. We hope our book will lead *you* into the life-enriching practice of daily writing.

Now, as you go into the exercises, we want to give you one main piece of advice. *Be loose!* (How else to say it? Be playful, if you can. Take chances. Or, to say it negatively, **Do not be too serious.**) Now that we've told *you* to be loose, we're reminded not to take ourselves too seriously. What nerve we have—setting ourselves up to help you be a poet!

"Poet." Is that a scary word? It is for some. When you write in the ordinary way, like this, you are a prose writer, and nobody gets uptight about being that. But what if you invite attention to your language by treating it in special ways—

with spaces   and glides, new

ways to begin lines, quick

ends, put in (say) a red barge, or silent

      dark butterfly, writing stuff-

that-looks-like-poetry?

Are you not then a poem writer? A poet? When we write in ways that invite attention to our language, we feel easy about saying, "I'm writing a poem." Even, "I'm a poet." We want you to feel easy too.

Getting the Knack will help you get the knack of poetry. If you haven't yet been where art is, in the quilts and songs, the sayings and thing-a-ma-bobs, it's hard to believe how easy art is—once you get the knack. Others use almost anything to make art. You'll be using words. When you practice enough that some of the language is really yours, you can get from it more than information, more than instruction. You can get to feelings—to your own and sometimes to others'. You will find your way to selected memories, and find ways to improve them. You will echo and music along into new areas no one before you has found.

That's right. Practice in writing and reading poems may lead you to your life. You just need to discover and enhance you knack.

We close this Foreward with a friendly wave to the dozens of students and teachers who tested our work and helped make it what it is.

And good luck.

Prelude

Come On In

You can't swim if you don't get in.

Writing is like that. You get the feel of it, and it takes you places you could never get any other way.

Try the shallow end first—pieces of language you might find and notice, fragments of headlines. Just dog-paddle around for awhile.

Then try the kind of writing everyone does: letters, recipes, little games. <u>The idea is that anyone can do it.</u> But even in the early pieces you begin to feel the current. It gets powerful—dreams grab you; you feel the kick and surge of forms.

Through the exercises that follow, any person, in a class or alone somewhere and wanting to experience how writing feels, can progress toward full participation. You have to want to do it though. We confess that. Or have a teacher who wants you to do it. Either way, the pages that follow will conduct you easily and surely forward. You can't fail. You may gasp a little now and then, but no one drowns, and everyone learns.

Come on.

Found & Headline Poems

Start here

A nice thing about "found" and "headline" poems: you don't start from scratch. All you have to do is find some good language and "improve" it.

How? You find interesting, ordinary "prose" (prose is language like this—not pretending to be poetry) and turn it into a thing-like-poem. We'll be more specific later on.

But first—this exercise gives us a chance to celebrate ordinary prose: its concreteness, its richness, and its surprises. In this exercise we're against fancy language. Words with too many syllables. Hollow words (such as "destiny" or "happiness") that can mean too many different things, and hollow titles for poems (such as "Feelings" or "Reflections"). We're against "poetic language," that is.

Plenty of strong and beautiful poems are made from plain language. You sometimes hear such language in conversation, when people are talking their best. Listen. Sometimes you yourself say wonderful things. Admit it. You can find moving, rich language in books, on walls, even in junk mail. (From such sources you'll probably find better poems, or better beginnings for poems, than from dictionaries and other word books.)

So, poems hide in things you and others say and write. They lie buried in places where language isn't so self-conscious as "real poetry" often is.

This exercise is about keeping your ears and eyes alert to the possibilities in ordinary language.

Not incidentally, it would be a good idea to start a poetry notebook. A place to collect your poetry stuff. As if you haven't already.

Found Poem Steps

Step 1.

Find from fifty to one hundred words you like. Words that really interest you. They may come all at once from one source—but they needn't. If you half-remember a good passage from a book or old magazine, track it down. Copy it. Check out mail, talk shows, walls, and malls. If you have a recorder, use it—but ask permission first. Hang around where people talk, where there's print. Eavesdrop—notebook and pencil ready for action. How much ordinary language? Fifty to one hundred words. That's not a whole lot. *This very paragraph is more than one hundred.* The key is to find interesting, good stuff.

It's probably easier to discover poems in printed materials than to try getting them through the ear, by hand, from conversations, televisions, or radios. Sure, some people who write fast or take shorthand can capture talk. Recorders do it better. We've read fine found poems recorded from a radio ministry, from speakers at a Martin Luther King celebration, and from hallway talk. Remember, get permission from persons you record. Found Poem poets have discovered good raw material in notices on bulletin boards and on highway maps; in insurance policies and in letters; in books, magazines, and newspapers. Obituaries yield good poems. So do some pieces of "junk mail." Old diaries.

Are those the only places?

No. Menus and notes left in desks. Historical plaques along the highways and classified ads. But while we're on *that* subject . . .

The **forbidden** sources are *poetry* and *song lyrics*. They're both already poetry. Stay away from commercial advertising and from other sources where the intent is to be "poetic."

But that prayer you heard? That letter from someone close? Ordinary or "poetic," it's up to you. The rule is: *Don't use language that has already been "artistically arranged,"* like song lyrics and billboards and new car ads.

And keep track of where you got your words so you can give the source credit.

Step 2.   (On scratch paper.) Copy the language in the sequence that you found it. Double space between lines so it's easy to work with.

Step 3.   Study the words you found. Cut out everything that's dull, or unnecessary, or sounds bad, or is otherwise offensive. Try to cut your original find in half—twenty-five words from the fifty you copied down, fifty from the hundred. *Change punctuation if you need to.*

But adding your own words to the found words is "illegal." Not tolerated in official Found Poem circles. A found poem is *found,* after all.

On the other hand . . . We've worked on found poems. We know how difficult it is. And we're easy. So how about . . .

When you're close to an edited-down version, and you truly need to add a word or two—to smooth things out, to make sense, to make a point—*you may add up to two words of your own.* Remember, that's two (2) words. Total. Make other *little* changes, too—tenses, possessives, plurals, punctuation, and capitalizations.

Step 4.   Read your cut-down draft one more time. Is there a better title than "Found Poem"? Put the words into your notebook, spacing or arranging them so they're poem-like. (Sometimes you will put key words at the ends or beginnings of lines. Sometimes, for interest or surprise, you may want to break up words that often "go together" [like "white clouds," by ending one line with "white" and starting the next line with "clouds."] Break lines so you emphasize key words, get good sounds at the ends of lines, or heighten the reader's interest.)

Here's our best advice: READ ALOUD AS YOU ARRANGE! Before you actually put the line on the page, test possible line ends by pausing ever-so-slightly at possible "breaks," or line ends. Reading aloud as you work will help you get lines that please you.

In short, if it sounds good, trust it.

Which line breaks seem to add most? Sometimes you'll want lines to end with natural phrases or ends of sentences. Other times you won't.

Arrange the words so they make a rhythm you like. You may

space   words   out   so   they   are   alone
or allruntogether.

Arrange them to read the way *you* like. You may want to put

key
words
on lines by themselves.

Or you may want to form the whole poem so it's fat, or skinny, or shaped like a polar bear.

People desperate to emphasize key words have been known to PRINT THEM LARGE, print them in colors, or underline them, use **different type faces** and even *italics*.

Your job is to arrange the language you found so as to enhance or improve it. To make it interesting, look good, and good to read.

At the bottom of the poem, tell where the words came from. Give credit. It's OK to borrow language for good uses like poem-making. But say where you found the original. For example, "From Chapter 2, *Huckleberry Finn*, by Mark Twain." Or "Overheard while waiting in line to check out at Kroger's."

As for a title, find one or make one up.

Step 5.   Well all right. If you began this exercise without a single poem in your pocket, you must be proud. You have found/shaped a thing-like-poem. That makes you a poet—maker of a thing-like-poem, at least.

In your notebook: *Enter a good copy of your thing-like-poem, signed.* (Extra credit: Carry around a copy of your poem and try to sneak it into casual conversation. Not easy, but not impossible.)

Here are found poems we like. Notice how "Wanted By Sheriff" is balanced on either side of an imaginary line running down its spine. And notice how "Prairie Wind" is arranged so the right side makes a straight vertical line.

Why are they arranged these ways?

Simply because we thought they looked good?

Text 1
Wanted by Sheriff

Wanted
By Sheriff, Muleshoe, Texas
Al Halstead
alias
Hal Alstead
Scheme: Mail order parts for
model cars—never
delivered.
Last seen leaving
Muleshoe
Texas
in white Cadillac
If found, inform Sheriff
Muleshoe,Texas.

(Found on the wall of the Post Office, Nickerson, Kansas.)

Here's a paragraph we found:

The plain spreads southward below the Trans-Canada Highway, an ocean of wind-troubled grass and grain. It has its remembered textures: winter wheat heavily headed, scoured and shadowed as if schools of fish move in it; spring wheat with its young seed-rows as precise as combings in a boy's wet hair; gray-brown summer fallow with the weeds disked under; and grass, the marvelous curly prairie wool tight to the earth's skin, straining the wind as the wheat does, but in its own way, secretly.   (83 words)

Text 2
Prairie Wind

Ocean of wind-troubled
grass. Winter wheat, scoured
and shadowed as if schools
of fish move in it. Spring wheat
seed-rows, combings in a boy's wet
hair. Curly prairie wool tight
to earth's skin, straining
wind, the girl's hair.   (38 words)

(From *Wolf Willow*, by Wallace Stegner)

Remember, we said, "you may add up to two words of your own"? "Girl's hair" are the two words we added.

Poems in Response

Today Men Are Mere Numbers

In mathematics we always look for a valid shortcut to
solving problems
Many physical and economic phenomena can be described
by exponential functions
A batted baseball
The tractor operator rotating the tire
An airplane flying ten pounds of mixed nuts
Interchange any 2 equations of the
Woman who invested her inheritance—
An unending line of dominos
We could knock down the entire line by knocking down
only one domino
A unique solution
The interchange of two rows
We could knock down the entire line by knocking down
only one man.

—Jennifer Plunk

(Found in *Precalculus* by Larson and Hostetler)

INVISIBLE DANCE

These are the mites,
Thousands and thousands of tiny mites:
Male mites and
Female mites and
Baby mites and
Even the mummified corpses
Of long dead old great-grandparent mites.

Brethren of theirs stir in the bed
Where they have spent the night snuggling
Warm and cozy.
Now beginning to stir for the day.

—Sharon Plavnick

(From *The Secret House* by David Bodanis)

Honey

Winnie-the-Pooh sat
at the _{foot} of the tree
        began to t-h-i-n-k
buzzing and
                buzzing and
                        buzzing
                "only reason for
                buzzing is
        you're a bee"
                "only reason for
        being a bee is making
HONEY!"
                "only reason for
making honey is so
I can eat it."

                                                        climbed
                                                and
                                        climbed
                                and
                        climbed
                and
        climbed
        and
Climbed
rather tired
$$\text{CRACK!}$$ (Oh help!)
dropped,
        fell,
                plummeted
flew gracefully into gorse-bush
"It all comes of
        liking HONEY
                so much!"

—Stephanie Anne Molnar
(from A. A. Milne's *Winnie the Pooh*)

In the North

The boy giggled quietly,
reaching out to touch a fawn
still red with camouflage spots,
walking out into the water
one careful step at a time,
stretching her nose to touch the finger
the boy was holding out.
Youngster meeting youngster.
Staged moment?
I have seen such a thing
from a canoe.

—Cris Anderson

(Words from *Woodsong* by
Gary Paulsen, 1990, p. 58)

The Same

Michael Gallatin was a large man
with
smooth grace
white strong teeth
long, lean legs
darkly handsome face
and
green eyes, a place of great danger.

The wolf was as big as a bull.
with
a body designed for special
white fangs
muscles rippled along its back
sleek black fur
and
same green eyes, danger

Both in one. . . .
werewolf

—Suzanne Gorrell

(From *The Wolf's Hour*
by Robert McCammon)

He's the **WARTIEST BOY**
trying to cure **WARTS.**
plays with frogs so much

the charm's **BUSTED!**

Take 'em off with a bean?
No.
Cure 'em with dead cats
'bout midnight
               at the
                       crossroads!

Jam your hand in—

That'll fetch any **WART**
and
pretty soon
               off
                     she

                     comes!

—Sangita Baruah

(From *The Adventures of Tom Sawyer*
by Mark Twain)

Personals

Come hula hoop
in the soft light
of a vintage 1928 armadillo lamp
in the swanky Bound Brook apartment
of this 26 year old
professional woman
who makes pumpkin pie
from scratch
and is able to converse
on a multitude of subjects.

—Stephanie Block

(From *The Medium*, The Rutgers
University Livingston
Campus Newspaper)

Indeed
there is an art

to
split
ting
in
fin
i
tive
s.

No point in m
angling
just
to
a(split)
void.

You are entitled
to
HAPPILY
go
to
HAPPILY
go
to
HAPPILY
go
a
head
and

S
P
L
I
T
!

—Donna-Marie Stupple
(From an article by Richard Lederer
"Good Usage *and* Good Taste"
Writer's Digest June 1991, p. 41)

Something

Something very odd in the farmlands
Strange circular depressions appear,
flattened
Puzzling circles pattern in a swirling leaving no clues

The search for answers
continues to ripen
ready for harvest.

Single rings linked by a long curling tail
Puzzling disturbances wild as a vicious wind
sculpting creations

SOMETHING is responsible.

—Mary Moebius
"Around and Around in Circles," Sally B. Donnelly, *Time*
magazine, September 18, 1989, p. 50

Headline Poems

The headline poem is a kind of found poem. You begin with words and phrases **found** and removed (by you) from a newspaper's headlines. You'll have plenty of pieces to work with. **Your main job is to discover and present—in an artistic and attractive way—connections in the language.**

Working on Texts 1 and 2 (above), we made decisions as to what words to keep, where best to end the lines, where to break for stanzas, how to punctuate, and what titles to give our work. The headline poem offers the same opportunities.

This could be a good time to work with others.

Three or four working together are not too many. Group work should be sociable, useful, and fun. Work with whom? Little brothers, friends, relatives, neighbors, parents, grandparents, maybe even with pets. Yes?

Solos are OK, too.

You'll also get help from the words themselves. You'll see.

Whether you work solo or with others, stay alert for surprises and connections among the words. Be playful, but beware! Words are independent cusses. They sometimes make connections on their own.

Headline Poem Steps

Step 1.

Cut out fifty or more words and phrases from one issue of a city newspaper. More is better, here. One hundred pieces are not too many. Keep the mutilated newspaper for later—in case you need a certain letter or word or punctuation mark. (If scissors work embarrasses you, do it where no one can see you.)

Most pieces should be individual words cut from longer headlines. As a rule, *don't use entire headlines*. Stay alert for good little words hiding in larger ones. Create new words by taping together parts of ordinary words. (We made "snarkles" out of "snacks" and "trifles." We made "camp-ramp" from "campers" and "ramp." Don't ask us why.)

Have some scissor fun.

Step 2.

Find a big clear surface to work on. Floors are good. Empty tables. Spread the pieces out and play. Move pieces around. Think about what you see. Read aloud individual pieces *and* other pieces that might connect.

Listen to the words. If a few of them seem to want to huddle, help them. Be open to strange connections. Be swift to embrace nonsense that makes you smile. **Don't let "sense" take over too early.**

As the poem settles down, continue to read aloud. Listen for sounds, rhythms, and connections you like. Listen also for good lines and for places to end lines. Test unpunctuated line ends by pausing briefly. Keep an ear open for a good line break.

Does a title come to mind? (Is there one hiding among the unused pieces?)

Step 3.   Find a sheet of paper of a size you like and lay out your words on the page. Do they fit? If not, remove some; trim others. (It probably looks better to have too few than too many words.) You may need to find extra letters (like *s*'s, or *ed*'s) or punctuation. (Now aren't you glad you saved the newspaper?)

Find and cut out what you need to make your poem complete. Then paste, staple, tape, or glue. (Optional: Decorate to taste.)

Step 4.   (Be patient. One step more.) Before you abandon your headline poem, read (on the following pages) the two we found. Both show influences and decisions that may interest you—for example, the alliterations in "<u>W</u>orkaday <u>W</u>orm": <u>L</u>ittle <u>l</u>eased <u>l</u>ashes. (Are there other alliterations?) Notice the arrangement of lines in "Bad News."

If it would please you to impose rhyme on your poem—rhyme at line ends or inside the lines—it's not too late. How about a formal pattern—alternating lines three and four words long? Or something else?

The tougher the task you impose on yourself, the sweeter the victory.

Sometimes.

In your Notebook: *Copy / paste / staple in your headline poem, the original or a copy.* At the bottom of your poem, for the sake of that person who will one day write your biography, write the name and the date of the newspaper you used.

Text 3

Workaday worm with

Little leased lashes

lures *legless* loon

with Gold go-go genes

to *draft* y disco.

Tax man

takes taxi-driver's tips.

Olympian mess
rendered with flair.

Text 4

Bad News

4 seal pups *mangle prayer book*

Religious volumes go fast

sanctuary Beavers romp,

Episcopalian editors

in moral crisis

sell church to neighbor

receive care

Poems in
Response

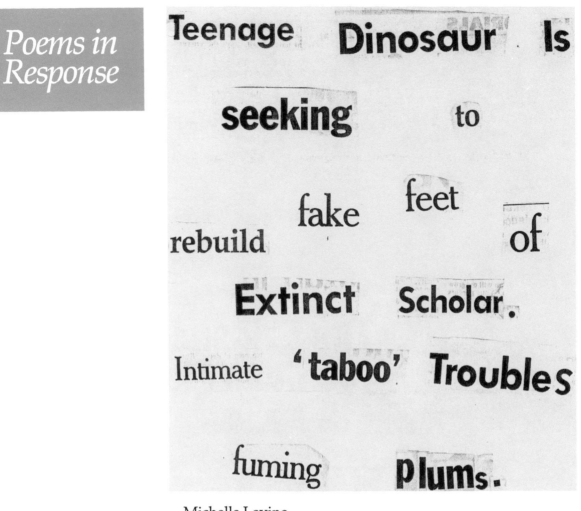

—Michelle Levine
San Francisco Examiner, May 12, 1991

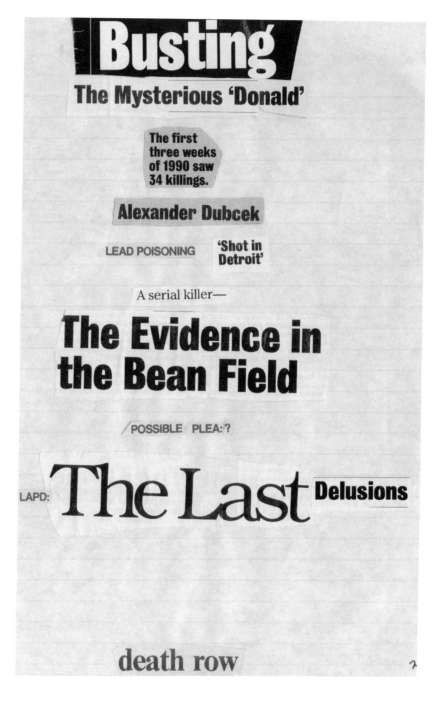

Busting
The Mysterious 'Donald'

The first three weeks of 1990 saw 34 killings.

Alexander Dubcek

LEAD POISONING   'Shot in Detroit'

A serial killer—

The Evidence in the Bean Field

POSSIBLE PLEA:?

LAPD: The Last Delusions

death row

—Brett Broussard

The boy's firm Father faced the two federal partners, and with his plentiful profits easily paid off the final PAYMENTS. The community Company came and caught the crime pair, and will send the men up North to put Penguins in ponds.

—Amanda LaFond
Star Tribune, May 3, 1991

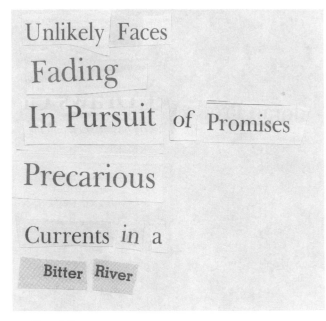

Unlikely Faces
Fading
In Pursuit of Promises
Precarious
Currents in a
Bitter River

—Carol Jago
The Christian Science Monitor, May 8, 1991

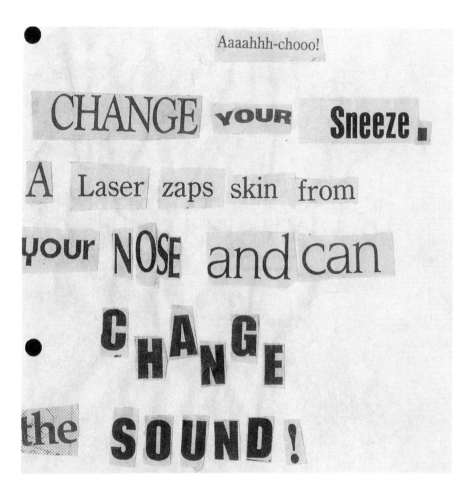

Aaaahhh-chooo!

CHANGE YOUR Sneeze. A Laser zaps skin from your NOSE and can CHANGE the SOUND!

—Vicki Bergeron
Chicago Tribune, May 19, 1991

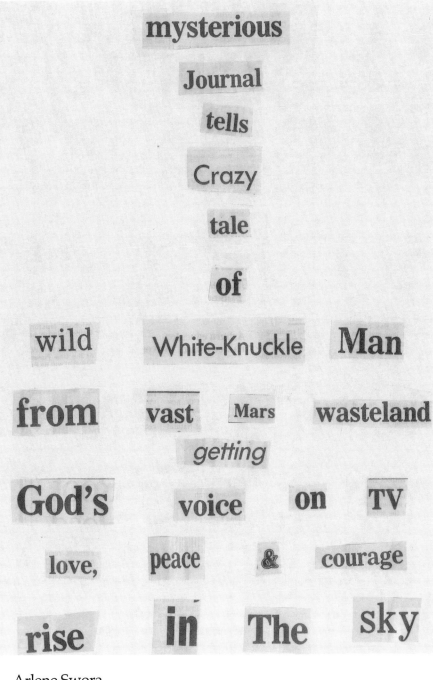

mysterious
Journal
tells
Crazy
tale
of
wild   White-Knuckle   Man
from   vast   Mars   wasteland
getting
God's   voice   on   TV
love,   peace   &   courage
rise   in   The   sky

—Arlene Swora
The Toledo Blade, May 10, 1991

It's time to leave

Flying cockroaches *spurn*

pastures of plenty, storm

secret luncheon party for Stanley

the sailor, found guilty

of Pitching Physical praise

at a *good* Woman,

who *took* off

for the Hills.

—William Burns
Detroit Free Press, May 15, 1987

Interlude

Letting Go of Other People's Language

You can find poems hidden in a text; you can take pieces of language and shift them around to create strange bits of reading, making the page look like a poem.

And once you see how easy that is, you can try out some language of your own—aiming to deliver a message, just telling someone something, as in a letter.

But before you do that, think back over what happened when you juggled pieces of headlines or arranged prose into a kind of a poem: you were forced into nonsense sometimes, or into what seemed like nonsense but then came to make a new kind of sense. That experience of strangeness is part of what liberates a writer. That freedom is precious: we don't always want to recast our writing—or our thinking—into old patterns. It is good to brainstorm, to write-storm.

Think of how someone around you will sometimes come up with a stunning new way of seeing, or of saying something. It's as if a door opens.

That wildness that comes from experiment can carry over, even into purposeful writing.

Letter Poems

Introduction

What do you already know about letter poems?

Plenty. You know how they begin. Like letters themselves, letter poems can start with a greeting, "Dear Somebody."

You know how they usually end—with some way of signing off: "Yours truly," or "Sincerely," or "Hang by your thumbs."

So in a sense, knowing about the letter poem's beginning and end, all you need worry about is the middle. Right?

Wrong. Probably the main qualities of letter poems come from who the letter is addressed to and who signs it. In ordinary letters, written to real people by real people, there's usually a known relationship. The writer (you) are writing a friend, a relative, an insurance agent. You and friend, relative, or insurance agent have a history, and that history shapes how the letter goes. "Dear Cousin Malcolm," it might begin, if it's to a cousin you've never met. "Malco-mio," if you've known him all your life.

Before you decide which letter poem to write, we want you to write drafts of three letters under rules somewhat different from the usual ones. You are not writing to make plans, or to exchange news, or to ask for something. You're writing to say something interesting, and to say it in a not-prose way.

Letter Poem Steps

Step 1.

On scratch paper, doodle around, putting down names of famous/ interesting people no longer alive. We thought of Queen Elizabeth I, Vince Lombardi, Booker T. Washington, Emily Dickinson, Adolph Hitler, Cochise, James Dean, Florence Nightingale, John Lennon, Bessie Smith . . .

Your list will be fresher. Try for eight or ten names.

Or maybe there's some "thing" or "force" out there that interests you. Wind, we thought of. Lightning. Dolphin. Shadow. Birch tree. Prejudice. Earth. Sweet-tasting things. Jot down four or five of these.

Then, too, there are living famous persons, breathing the very air we breathe. Performers, social workers, athletes, dreamers. In another place on your page, name a few famous/interesting persons alive today.

Now look over all the names on your page. If you could write to only one of those persons or things, who or what would it be?

Step 2. Draft a letter to that name. One page maximum. It will begin:

Dear_____ ,

In your letter, tell_____who you are and what's on your mind. Do you want advice? To ask questions about her/his/its life or situation? To straighten her/him/it out on a few matters?

Serious or silly? Distanced or intimate? It's up to you.

In this draft, when you talk about yourself (or write "I"), **the real you is talking.** Reveal some things, if you dare. Get close to real feeling.

Sign your real name at the bottom.

Here's an example of a letter we wrote to a baseball pitcher named Art Herring who played for the St. Paul Saints in the 1930s.

Text 5

Dear Art Herring,

My mean cousin Rhonda was acting a little weird at the family reunion last week, asking would I rather be you, Willie Mays, or President. Rhonda and I were at that game where you set a record— hitting four consecutive doubles. That was the day Rhonda swiped my root beer, my hot dog, and said she'd break my arm if I told.

Rhonda and I haven't gotten along these past fifty years.

Even so, I answered truly I'd rather be you, and I would. *The only time I've seen history made* was the day you hit those four beauties. Also, you were a saint to us kids. Twice you signed programs, once you gave me a ball.

Want to see it?

Please answer one question. You were a pitcher, and got those four doubles. But most pitchers can't hit a lick. WHY IS THAT?

Rhonda says you won't answer. But I get dinner on her if you do.

Your fan,

Stephen Dunning

Step 3. On scratch paper, draft a letter as if it were written **by** a famous person or thing. Maybe the names you jotted earlier will give you the right famous writer. But this would be a good time to add names: Whose letter would you really like to read?

Finally, of course, you have to choose one writer—Mother Teresa, Winter of '91, Rudolph Valentino, Moon. And once the writer is set, you must decide who's going to receive it.

That recipient could be you yourself. If you want to hear from somebody/something famous, here's your chance.

Say that your name is José McNulty. The letter might begin:

Dear José,

It will be signed by the famous person/thing of your choice.

There's another possibility. What if some famous person/ place/thing, living or dead, wrote to another "ditto"? An opera great from the past writes to a young singer debuting at the Met? General Lee to General Schwartzkopf? Elizabeth Barrett Browning writes to a poet whose first book has just been reviewed in the *Times?*

You should know something about the person/thing who will write this next draft. But decide who writes, who receives.

It might be best to start the letter as if it were one letter in an ongoing series between the writer/receiver. In that case, it could begin *in medias res*—in the middle of things, e.g., *Dear Freddie, What do you mean, bacon?*

Step 4.   Draft a letter written by that famous person/thing. One page or less. Here's one we received just the other day.

Text 6

Dear William Stafford:
    You ask me to analyze your dream, the one
in the open where the animals ran and something
else ran. Hoofs went loss, loss, loss, and
the muscles that would die snorted strong.
    What those things were, in your dream,
they were horses.
    You will receive a bill for my usual fee.
                                    Sincerely,
                                    Sigmund Freud

Step 5.   If you dare, bring true feelings into this third draft, and write it to someone or something you really care about. *Draft a letter to someone known to you but not to us, or to something you know in a special way.* A neighbor. A teacher. That river near your home. Someone/something you'd like to meet, or know better. Someone you don't want to associate with any longer. Tell this person specific things. *Instead of* "I like you," *try* "Your smile is quick, and I like the way your nose goes off to one side." *Not* "I hate you," *but* "What you said about Asians made my heart ache."

So that you feel free to write "close to the bone," sign this draft with someone else's name. Use "Anonymous," if you don't think of anything better.

Express affection, fear, curiosity, or hope. Outrage or gratitude, pride or shame. *The feelings should be your own, the person you write them to should be someone who matters to you, but the name you sign should not be your own.* We've seen important letters signed by "Ophelia," "The Girl in the Swing," and "The Apostle Luke." We've seen others signed more anonymously, by "Just Hoping," and "A Friend Who Cares."

Here's an example of what we mean:

Text 7

Dear Husband,

I write *Personal* on the envelope.
Someone else opens and reads

The letter I meant only for you.
First time in a month we take
Time for wine in a bar. Your
Briefcase sits between us; you
Touch papers in your pockets,
Scrunch your eyes, look around.
At work, the operator won't put
Me through to you. You are in
Conference, in Cleveland, in-
Communicado. You never call
Back. Dear distracted executive
Husband of mine, your doors are
Closed. You're hiding. Come out.

Your Very Worried Wife

—Dorothy Schieber Miller
and Stephen Dunning

Step 6. Choose from your drafts the one you like most, and work on it. ("Work on it" *how?*)

Letter poems draw attention to themselves by looking different from regular letters, by being as much concerned with imagined things as real things, and by their language.

So far we've called our drafts "letters." What must we do to them before we call them "letter poems"?

Not too much. Try these four ways of revising.

A. Squeeze the draft you've selected. Look in every sentence for unnecessary words and phrases. Find places you can substitute one or two new words for three or four old. Cut whole chunks. Cut *to* the good stuff.

B. At a point or two where you have language you like, say more. Start the "expansion" with words like "as if." In Text 5, "My mean cousin Rhonda was acting a little weird at the family reunion last week" might first be cut ("Rhonda got weird") and then expanded with examples:

Rhonda got weird, as if baseballs were potato
salad and Cousin Lou was out at home.

C. Are the parts of your draft in the best order? Read it to see. Shift parts around, making whatever other changes such shifting requires. Keep an eye out for chunks that might be shuffled out altogether.

D. Read *aloud* as you work and find interesting places to end lines. In regular letters, lines extend to the right hand margin:

(out to here➜)

Letter-poem poets end lines where they want—where they sound and look best, give the most lift. End several lines with words that have sounds in common. For us, "soun<u>d</u>" rhymes with "brea<u>d</u>," and "l<u>ean</u>" rhymes with "s<u>ee</u>d." (And, yes, "cat" rhymes with "mat.")

Go more for our partial kinds of rhymes.

Step 7.   Work over your letter poem, cutting, expanding, rearranging as you go. **In your notebook:** *rework your letter poem into your notebook.*

(Extra credit: if your letter poem is frankly GREAT, send it to someone, living or dead. Or tack it to a tree, so anyone can read it.)

Poems in Response

Dear Polluted Lake,

I see you struggle each day
Trying to push filth away;
Pushing bloated fish towards shore
Not wanting garbage dumped anymore!
Boats travel with empty brains at their wheel
As they toss cans and papers for your meal.
My dear friend, I miss our silent talks
Or those calming meditative walks.
I miss just sitting at your side
Soaking my feet while I confide
About all my worries and hopes
and now—
            I have to wonder . . .
                        Is there any hope
                                    left
                        for you?

Your worried Friend

                        —Lorri LM Goodall

Dear Roadrunner,

I wish that someday I
could meet you in person.
I love to watch as you outsmart
and outrun the Coyote.
Where do you sleep?
Do you have a family?
What else do you do
besides run around all day?
We should have lunch.
What <u>do</u> roadrunners eat?
One last question—
if you had a race with Speedy Gonzalez
who would win?

Your Biggest Fan

                        —Andrea Siegrist

To all nail polish name inventors

It has been brought
to my attention
all the intricate,
imaginative words
you people can invent
for ordinary colors.

"California Sunshine"?
"Ripe Apple"?
"Fire Alert"?
"Pumpkin Pie"?
"Shimmer Ice"?
"Creamy Pear"?
And my personal favorite,
"Faux Pearles"!

I commend your creativity,
but with all the
            brainstorming you
 must go through,
 it would be my
 guess you could
 get a better job!
 Please respond and
 give me the insight
 on your career.

                    Sincerely,

                Lori Morency

P.S. May I suggest "Red"? "Pink"?

                —Lori Morency

TO MY GREAT UNCLE

You tilted back and carved a plug.
Your blade was sharp and mirror bright.
You worked the plug into your mouth,
Your cheeks inflating like an adder's.

Your ancient eyes were gray and piercing.
Thinning was your wild and tangled hair.
With ankle perched on knee, you rubbed
From thigh to wounded toe and said:

"The bull stomped on that toe and tore
It up. The damnfool doctor said
It'd never heal. Now look at it—
A scab already. Nothing like
Tobacco juice to heal a sore."

With that you spat an amber stream
on that swollen, mangled toe.

"What a fool I was to go
To doctors: if a man's eighteen
and don't know how to cure himself
he's a fool and ought to die
Anyway."
YOUR HYPOCHONDRIACAL NEPHEW

                    —James S. Mullican

Dear E.A. Poe,

You fascinate me.
Were you whacko?
Your killer in <u>The Tell Tale Heart</u>
Actually loved that old man!
Montresor got away with it.
Yeahhh!!!
But didn't his basement stink?
Don't fret over Lenore.
If the angels named her,
She can't have been much fun.
Stick with that bird.
He sounds smart.
As for Annabel Lee,
Get a life, Edgar—
Quit sleeping in sepulchers.
People do talk.
Please R.S.V.P. my invitation.
I'm anxious to see you.
So's my sister.
                    Roderick Usher

          —Sister Brigid O'Donoghue

Dear Dolphin,

I wish my skin as tight as yours
no more clam grey but liquid silver
a svelte velvet caressing the water

I wish my body, a curvaceous
flexible flyer, cracking the surface
without breaking a bone

oh dolphin, you have no smile lines
or widow's peak or perpetual frown,
you can stay down

and, come back up again—
how many can boast of that?
to live in the earth's amniotic womb—

move over, is there room?

                              An Aquatic Admirer

                                   —Nancy Gorrell

Dear Homeowner

At four a.m.
Lie awake and listen.
We are in sleepers and joists
Chewing the interest
Before you reach the equity.

The termite inspector
Didn't really look
Hurried home to Saturday night
And you signed the sale.
Now the damage runs six grand.
Litigation lingers.

So do we.

In dark moist mud we mingle
Salute the queen and surge
Upward until we arrive
At the second floor bedroom.

In the morning
On pale new paint
You will find
The collection of crusty dots
Pin-head sized.

Brush them away.
Stare into the tiny cavities.
We are here.

Termites subterranean
Yours

    —Pamela Merideth

Dear Tomorrow:

See your animals fade away
Like the night at dawn.
Watch the leopard's fur
Being used for show.
See the king of beasts,
The bravest one,
Run for cover
At the noise of the hunter's gun.
Watch the ruthless killers
Grow greedy and rich.
They seem more like an enemy
Than a friend.
See the animals die poor
Just as before.
Yet they are still beautiful
As more and more
They fade away.

Yesterday

    —Julie Patten

Dear Nature,

 Your anger is of no
surprise.
 I don't understand how
our children can treat
us like a gigantic trash
can and barren wasteland.
 I sympathize with
your position, and I
realize the dangers you
face.

But remember,
Like that which consumed
the dinosaur, I too am in
danger of rapid extinction.
    Pray for those trying
to heal us.
    Hope for the best;
and get some rest, for
tomorrow you will
need your strength.

                              Mother Earth

                        —Tracy Valstad

Dear Queen Anne Boleyn,

I'm surprised to hear of
Your marriage to King Henry VIII.
I never thought you were
Power hungry.
If you love him
Be careful
He's cruel and
Bores easily.
While you will stay true
He will chase after
Any pretty face.
Please be careful.

                        Your loyal subject,
                        Arielle Siebert

                        —Arielle Siebert

Dear Melissa,

        I've been sitting in this
cage day and night. I'm getting
bored. The most excitement I get is to
run around aimlessly, in this
wheel—which is due for a lube
job. Every once in a while, I see
the outside of my cage, only to be
placed into another. (Loads of fun!)

My point is you can let me out of
my cage, at least once in a blue moon,
to roam around your room. I'm
small and not as quick as you
may think. (Watch my dust fly!) So,
can we work something out?
      I better get back to my wheel—
the quarter is about to run out in
the meter.
      By the way, while I'm on the
subject, can we discuss the topic of
menu?

           Your "captive" friend,

           Tippy the Hamster

             —Melissa Oxley

Dear Claudia,
      You caught me unaware
by bringing "Carlo" Williams into class
for your report. He stood
out from the mob of poets
I knew more of than my students.

      You caught me yet again
by giving birth to student poems
where only high school tabloid news had been.
I thought, therefore, that nothing
you achieved thereafter would surprise.

      Until one day white ducks on Highway 2
caught a driver unaware in front
and one behind—as deafeningly
your scarlet petals bloomed—

      You taught me unaware

      So much depends . . .

      So much.

           Sincerely,

           Mr. K.

             —Dave Korkowski

Interlude

From Letter to Literature

When you reach out toward someone, as in a letter, you take aim, you know something of the person who will be reacting. How does this help? Well, in thinking about your audience you have to examine your own ideas; so maybe you gain, as in a dialogue when another person adds to the life of language.

But in order to appeal to someone you may depart from your own best self. Does that make you disguise true feelings? Do you always just say what you think or feel? If you change for the purpose of persuading, are you dishonest? Can you be yourself, truly, even when considering the effects of what you say?

This kind of question can haunt all your writing (and talking) (and acting or being). Further writing can exercise that part of you that considers such things. But don't go too fast; try out some forms, like those that follow. Don't get into deep water too soon.

Acrostic & Recipe Poems

Acrostic Poems

Is it too late to say. . . ?

Sometimes, as you're slaving away on one of our exercises, your work may develop ideas of its own. Some formal notion may come up—about stanzas, say, or sounds. About line lengths or rhythms. Our advice is **Pay Attention.**

(You mean even if my poem veers off from the exercise?)
YES! That's OK. It could be terrific.
When in doubt . . .
"Abandon our exercise; follow your poem."

Here's something else: What a poem is/says depends partly on its form. Take **the acrostic**—So far, the forms in our exercises are more playful than traditional. Remember? We asked you to write a letter poem but not a sonnet.

Now we're asking for acrostics and recipes—but not for sestinas or odes.

The acrostic begins with a word or phrase written vertically downwards. The listed letters become the first letters in a string of words.

Take the astrological sign "Scorpio." You "list it" and "fill out the form" with one word for each line:

<u>S</u>uffering
<u>c</u>atfish,
<u>O</u>livia!
<u>R</u>elocating
<u>p</u>enguins
<u>i</u>n
<u>O</u>regon?

If your sign were Leo, your string of words would be different:

<u>L</u>eopards
<u>E</u>at
<u>O</u>nions   (Leo's so short! We'll just keep going . . .)
<u>L</u>ike
<u>E</u>ngineers
<u>O</u>rder
<u>L</u>asagna:

<u>E</u>thiopian
<u>O</u>lives
   (We could go on forever. Uh, anyone got a good "L"?)

Both the acrostic and recipe forms help shape the poem from "the outside." The shape is there from the start. The forms are external, driving the language and meaning. But . . .

Another kind of form can develop as you're making such poems. This kind, what we'll call "internal form," is more important. Unlike a form that already exists (for instance, haiku or sonnet), this kind develops from inside.

And each poem is different.

It's as if you discover internal form as you're working. You're writing along and you notice things happening in the language. Certain sounds occur—the "k" sound, say, or the low "oo." You wonder why. Maybe lots of white shows up—sheets, snow, a white fence, the skin on the inside of Monica's wrist. Hmmm. Then you notice that a visual pattern seems to be asserting itself—two short lines, then a long one. Hmmm again.

Is the poem trying to tell you something?

Should you help it become what it wants to be?

Form that emerges in the making interests us. Yet we ask for "external" forms? How come?

Because, at their best, such forms as acrostics and recipes invite exploring more than telling, ask more for "discovering" meaning than for delivering it.

We're partial to poems that *explore* and *ask* rather than *tell*. We believe that if we practice poem-writing attentively and openly and often, we might bump into angles worth sharing. <u>As might you.</u>

The acrostic and recipe poems start with little external structures—a word spelled down the page, a little formula. These "givens" help you generate language. On a good day, with a favorable wind at your back, you may encounter language you like and, even, "internal" clues that tell you how the poem itself wants to look and sound. Pay attention.

Acrostic Poem Steps

Step 1.

Doodle a string of words from your own astrological sign (as we did with "Scorpio"). Or start from your name, or your pet's, or from your birth-month, or the name of the city where your true love lives, or . . .

Salvatore is a longer name than *Joe*. If the word you choose has only three or four letters, play fair: Repeat such short words at least once, or put other words with them (Joe Joe, or Joe Palumbo).

Step 2.

Think up an important word (like <u>spaghetti</u>) or phrase (like <u>The cat's pajamas</u>) or name (like <u>Marlene</u> or <u>Peoria</u>) and list it vertically down the left side of a page. Again, you will use the letters of your acrostic word(s) as the first letters of lines. But this time, let the line be as many words long as it should be.

For example, a <u>one-word-per-line</u> acrostic on <u>spaghetti</u> might begin

> <u>S</u>ixteen
> <u>p</u>eppers
> <u>a</u>ctually
> <u>g</u>rew . . .

But a <u>longer-line</u> acrostic might begin

> <u>S</u>undays her mother felt the
> <u>p</u>owerful force of loss
> <u>a</u>s she minced Melissa's
> <u>g</u>arlic, rubbed coarse salt . . .

Step 3.   On scratch paper, write first drafts of *at least* three more acrostics—single-word or longer-line. Start with words that sound good to you, words that interest you and connect with you. Look especially for thematic or topical connections between the word(s) you set down vertically and the words you generate from it.

Poems in Response

SERENDIPITY

Seeing
Elephants
Riding
East
Never
Did
Inspire
Poets
In the least
To
Outloudly
Utter
Serendipity

—Diane Lockward

How I Avoided Doing My Acrostic Poem
                          or
What One Does When One Has
                          No Ideas

Prepare to write
Relax and think
Organize desk
Critique contents
Rearrange desk materials
Aim to begin
Select and list words
Trim unnecessary ones
Intuit and intuit
Nurture every scrap
Align words in rows
Tear them up
Inspire self with peanut butter sandwich
Organize desk
Nap on couch

                          —Nona Horsley

Musing over details of
Yet another murder near Victoria
Station, Inspector Morse reviewed the
Twelve suspects,
Each well-alibied and professionally above
Reproach,
Yet one gruesomely psychopathic.

—Dave Korkowski

The Turning

Suddenly, in this month of celebrations, a birthday—
  utterly and undeniably yours.
Maybe, on this longest day, you'll stay up,
  meet tomorrow morning, and she will show you how
Early everything begins,
  rises, and how late everything else
Sets. My friend—you have been sunrise
  on top of sunset, a strawberry moon
Lying low across
  strawberry fields.
This is the season of summer fruit, flowers,
  insects. Let us
Cool and comfort each other,
  early and late.

—Anna McEwen

Climbing gently at first,
Lissome, lithe as any acrobat, the clematis,
Espaliered against the gray lamp post,
Makes its lush way to the top.
Animated tendrils pick up speed as they wire their way to the
                          lantern where
Tissue-thin blossoms, huge and trembling,
Issue wildly forth in a glorious
Spill of velvet-fringed violet.

—Bonnie Jean Cousineau

The Naval Academy

As soon as the
Naval Academy
Negated the
Axiom allowing
People
Only of the
Lower gender of males
In, my
Sister decided to go.

—Stephanie Anne Molnar

Allison

As she sits silently, and
Listens to the classic music of the
Lucid rain drops, chattering
Importantly amongst each other,
She sighs warmly, pulling an
Old afghan over her, dreaming about
New purple mauve ideas.

—Allison Boye

    Anemona are
a Nathema to their
   Enemies, and
   More
s O to their
   Naughty
progEny.

—Michael Behrman

Fumbling for words,
Long, windy breaths,
Anxiety accentuating
Bulbous
Bug-
Eyed stares,
Raging emotions,
Gullible disbelief,
Astounded ignorance of
Something
Too
Extraordinary to be
Divulged.

    —Sundee Raudabaugh

Dancing through dreams,
Awakened by the
Never-ending music.
Catching the sky
In one tremendous leap.
Now soaring powerfully, while
Grasping for the stars.

    —Amy Waller

Recipe Poems

By *recipe poems* we mean cooking recipes, rules, and directions. In a sense, a recipe *is* a set of rules:

> To do this (make chicken soup, say), do this (boil water); then do this (add a carrot); and this is the result (soup).

Text 8

Recipe for School-type Chicken Soup

Into a friendly saucepan pour
One gallon water. Slice and add
One splendid carrot. Toss in a cupful
Of handsome rice and bring the whole mess
To a boil. Simmer for an hour.
Or simmer for two if you are *occupado*
With algebra or Mike. Cast
A scatter of salt atop the water's
Dancing face. For flavor add leftover
Chicken wing. Whatever it is, it serves six.

What keeps the recipe poem moving is external form—first, the title, telling exactly what the recipe is for; then, what ingredients are needed, and how to prepare and combine them; finally, how to serve what you've made.

Need the recipe poem be for food? No. Nor need it be silly.

Text 9   . . . With the leftovers and etcetera of the poor
we can build a skeleton—
chicken bones and gruel (for glue)—
and perhaps the remains
of a slim cat on a skewer
for the spine.
Does anyone have a heart
for the heart we need
to give the skeleton feelings?

(From Stephen Dunn's "Building a Person")

So, recipe poems can be thought of as recipe-like sets of rules—like rules you might make for a backyard volleyball game: "Claude's book-bag there is out of bounds"—and also as recipe-like directions, as in "Building a Person."

Recipe Poem Steps

The recipe structure is strong, and often helps writers generate language. In other exercises we expect you to find your meanings and forms as you work. The recipe poem works best if you know from the start *what your recipe is for.*

Step 1.   To find a subject that interests you, brainstorm topics or ideas; for example:

(a) steps to follow in assembling some magic thing

(b) how to cure sadness

(c) getting off LJ's bad-people list

Write your brainstorming ideas as titles for directions, recipes, or rules:

(a) How to Assemble HI-FLI Magic Carpet

(b) Mother Murgatroyd's Home Recipe for Curing the Blues

(c) Rules to Follow During Lovers' Quarrels

Try for five or more possibilities.

Step 2.   On scratch paper, write down your best title. Follow it with a recipe-like list of five or more steps. Each step, whether you're doing a recipe, instructions, or rules, should combine *actions* with *ingredients:*

(a) Weave 3 threads labeled GOLD and 4 threads labeled SILVER through the woof—or is it the warp?

(b) Mix six notes from the E-flat alto sax
with broth of juniper juice.

(c) Whisper her name to the left, to the right
        And (grinning) straight at her heart.

Step 3.   At the end of your list, answer some question like "So what?" For the
                examples above, the "so what's" might be:

(a) HI-FLI Magic Carpet is ready to fly. Enjoy your journeys.
        With proper care and good winds, HI-FLI may last forever.

(b) Sprinkle with nutmeg & munch at lunch. Serves four.

(c) LJ's arms will open like petals.

Step 4.   **In your Notebook:** Revising as the spirit moves you, *write a new
                version of your best acrostic* or *recipe draft.* (If both are pure dynamite,
                enter both.)
                (Extra credit: Find and copy a good poem. Give it to someone
                you like. In your Notebook, write down two or three things you
                notice about that fine poem.)

Poems in Response

Phoenix

Take a fresh week in the woods.
Clean carefully—
      plucking mosquitos,
      deer flies,
      wood ticks—
      (drown these in one pint
      grain alcohol and reserve.)
Wrap flesh lightly in flannel.

Add –three or four long walks
    (narrow trails overgrown in
    blueberries add color and flavor).

    – a dash of thrush song
    – the flutter of bat wings
    – an owl hoot
    – a whiff of skunk (if desired)

Let rest in shade until sunset.

    Then . . .

Place ingredients in covered cast iron pot.

Bake by slow campfire several hours.
    (Do not peek. Soon enough
    it will be done!)

Refuel as necessary.
    (Branches of fallen maple
    atop split logs of oak
    send upward a heavenly smoke.)

When coals glow, flameless,
    Open reserve, and upon them
    pour ablution for
    the dying day.

Savor.

                      —Janice Byrne

Recipe for Rain

Assume a plucked-string of tension
From the closed-eye lips
Of a breathing leaf.
Shudder with a baby's breath of whispers,
A fern's hush of moisture.
Cream with moonlit twilight
And sprinkle over wilted heat.

—Megan Grumbing

Uncle Sam's Own Recipe
For Well-Done Societies

Obtain a large chunk
of soil (ideally stretching
sea to shining sea).
Sprinkle generously with
assorted people,
aspirations, histories,
and intents.
Congeal with a
broad, representative
government.
Blend together smoothly
with mass
communications.
Stir occasionally using
overseas expansion,
big business, or
domestic turmoil.
Cover with corruption
and censorship
and let simmer.
Let off steam
with impeachment
and keep the flame
burning low.
Makes a fabulous
centerpiece at the
feast of nations.

—Brett Broussard

Finding a Friend

First we need a heart,
          a loving, kind heart.
Next we need some trust,
          a non-betrayal trust.
After that we need a mind,
          an extra-understanding mind.
Add a dash of salt and pepper,
          along with many spices.
Mix these until blended well.
This concoction will become a friend
          to all she meets.
Remember it's a friend you have,
          to love and care for.

—Shelly Muza

Carry a Morning Glory

across state lines. Find an old soup
spoon, dig up roots
the plant is yours
to coddle. You must make him shelter,
perhaps newspaper folded into a bed
a tent or a cone. Remember,

your tenant is terrified. Ease
him in, promise a white
trellis, fat worms, good sun.
Let water drop
from your fingers like rain.
Provide backseat shade,

then follow morning out of town.
Who ever said you can't package
and transport glory?

—Deborah Bayer

A Surenough Way To Get Depressed On Saturday Night

Retreat to one dark bedroom,
Taking with you a carton of Rocky Road and a bag of pretzels.
Select some appropriate mood music (suggestion: Johnny
Mathis).
Ask your favorite pillow to dance and don't forget to . . .
Convince yourself that the one you love is never coming back.

From here it can only get better!

—Jenny Jernberg

Sure Fire Directions From Here to There

Pull out of the crumbling tar parking lot. Be careful
of people, horses and cats. Turn right at the
stop sign. If there is no sign, go straight forward.
At the birthplace of the author of Mainstreet, take
the highway going east. Continuing until you hit the
Cities. Take the third exit, going south. Drive until
past where one airplane crashed and turn right before
where another plane crashed. At the end of the street,
a blue house with a rock in the front where three
drunks got their car hung up. That is my home.
Maybe it is your house too.

—Meredith McGrath

How to Make Your Mom Mad

FIRST, you talk on the phone.
talk on the phone so long
until you hear the SIMMER
of your Mom's voice—
THEN hang up!
ADD her favorite earrings to your lobes,
they look pretty with your jeans . . .
but if you hear her scream,
REMOVE THEM QUICKLY
you won't want her to BOIL over into wrath.
Just make her a little mad
at her favorite daughter, Cath.

—Donna L. Clovis

How to Prepare a Soft-Shelled Crab for Grandmother

Go in a silent boat on a full-moon night.
Follow the low tide banks, peer with your lantern
into hollows. There! A motion! A flash of claw,
a crawl of mud. Slowly reach beneath it with your net.
Then, in one swift motion, lift!

The guardian snaps and threatens.
Release him into a galvanized pail. Feel
into the clump of netted mud and gently, gently
take into your hand the newly molted crab.
Rinse in the salty water that holds the boat.

Grandmother will be waiting. In the kitchen,
with a small sharp knife, make the critical cut,
a semi-circle in tender shell beneath the eyes.

While oil heats in the heavy pan,
roll the crab in corn meal.
Place it hissing in the oil, its soft claws folded
to its body. Fry golden, first on one side
then the other. Serve with grits. Enjoy
grandmother's toothless celebration.

—Anne McCrary Sullivan

Cooking Summer

When the grove grows long
and shadows tease the heat,
spread out twilight with a gentle breeze.
Sprinkle in a handful of sunburned sisters
a cupful of lemon lit fireflies.
Gently toss to the cadence of cricket and cicada
and squealing, dancing daughters.
Blend into the darkness.
Serve up a whisper to the summer
moon, peeking through the oaks, and sigh
for it to last,
"just a little longer."

—Margaret Finders

How to Snare Romance

Walk toward the eastern horizon at sundown.
Turn suddenly, taking care to align your heart
With the streaked sky before you.
Imagine the sun balanced on a distant treetop
So far away your eyes can never see though your heart
Knows the leaves, the bark, the number of rings.
Take a step to your right
For everyone you have loved
And a step forward
For everyone who has loved you. At the end
Of your steps, turn again, suddenly, completely, eyes closed.
Open your heart.
Open your eyes.
You will be found soon.

—Randall Heeres

HOW TO COACH A T-BALL TEAM

Bandage the cut Kyle got riding his bike to practice.
Listen attentively to Ryan, who has to pee.
Remove Anthony's finger from his nose 3 times.
Explain to the squirming Ryan that there are no restrooms
        at this park.
Make sure none of the 7 identical Ninja Turtles water bottles
        get mixed up.
Explain why the coach of the green team got mad when
            Stephen
        ran from Home plate to second, then first, third, and
        Home. (But he went to all the bases!)
Listen when Kevin tells you you are the best coach ever.
        ("Way better than Mr. Hoffman. When I asked him
            what
        time it was he always said 'Time to pay attention.'")

—Christine Kolaya

Interlude

Cutting Loose

Now comes the good part.

Those early exercises were OK. The idea was to limber up with writing that everyone easily does, using common patterns like addressing a friend in a letter. But now we intend to venture on from word games toward spontaneous lines that may even spring from the wild country of dreams.

Now your own material and your own forms will be primary.

At least so it seems. But part of that self you will be relying on can use some of the surprises that word games keep on inviting you to notice. We are still flirting with that dividing line between the unedited flow of thought and the interesting changes that outside requirements can force on you.

Bring along that recklessness—**onward.**

Dream-Write 1

Introduction

Dreams are a good source of poems. Like many good poems, dreams are unplanned and wild and sometimes scary. They follow a logic all their own. We've never heard anyone say dreams are dull.

Some writers keep "dream books." They get up early and write down what they remember of their dreams. But dream memory is fragile and short. Have you ever awakened, remembering a dream, sure that the dream's vivid details will stay in mind?

Then POOF! The dream's gone, or remembered only in general.

Some people are at ease talking about dreams—telling theirs to friends. Others keep their dreams to themselves, not sure they *should* be shared. Some people are embarrassed by the content of dreams.

Do we hear someone saying, "But I don't dream"?

Almost surely that person is wrong. "I don't remember my dreams" is closer to the truth. Dreams help keep us healthy. People deprived of sleep (and thus of dreams) can become irritable and sick. We are all dreamers.

If you remember dreams well, start writing them down. If you awaken from a dream, try to write it down then. Keep a notebook and pen near your bed, under your pillow even. You may need a light to write legibly enough that you'll be able to read it later. If where you sleep is dark, try to find a night-light, or borrow a flashlight.

In truth, if we thought you could keep a dream journal, and that you ***would***, *we wouldn't bother with dream-write.* But some persons who remember dreams aren't about to share them with strangers. With us. Others aren't about to write down all that incriminating dream evidence. And to tell the truth, some feel that they get up early enough as it is.

Dream-write is a substitute for dream journals, a way of producing language and images that often occur naturally through dreams. The reason for going to all the trouble of dream journals or dream-writes is that the "material" or "stuff" that can come out of these processes is special. *You can't "think" or "imagine" your way to it.*

OK. We call this exercise Dream-write, but that's mainly so you'll know our aim. That aim is **to get you to produce unedited, uncensored, dream-like raw material.** You can approximate the "material" of real dreams by writing *fast*. Dream-write means fast-write. Not something like "free-write," as you may have practiced in keeping diaries and journals. Not pretty fast, or simply faster than you usually write. But fast as the wind. So fast that you stumble and make mistakes and write more nonsense than sense.

Perhaps for what we want "fast-write" is a more accurate term than "dream-write." But we'll stick with dream-write as a reminder of what it is we're after—those wild, surreal things called dreams.

Dream-Write Steps

Step 1.

Find a partner to work with. This work won't take long. Someone at school, a friend, someone where you live—*anyone* willing to help. You'll need scratch paper and something to write with. If you have access to a word processor, that will do just fine. You'll also need a watch with a second hand or a place to work where you can see the second hand of a clock. A stop watch would be *muy bueno*.

Step 2.

Your aim is to write as many words as possible. Thus, groups of words work better than individual words or lists. Writing individual words—<u>chalkboard, table, aisle, smell</u>—is slower than writing groups (or phrases)—<u>the chalkboard above the table at the end of the aisle, something smells like old closet.</u> Also, when writing word groups, you "get credit" for all the little words—the, above, at, *et cetera*.

Keep your pen or pencil on the page. Don't print, unless you print faster than you write. When you're ready to dream-write, have your partner say, "Ready," then "Set," then "Go."

Your partner should stop you *after exactly one minute* of furiously fast writing.

Step 3.

Label that "Dream-write 1." (Keep each dream-write on a separate page.) Count how many words it has, and put that number in a circle at the end. We hope you wrote swiftly.

But listen! What's fast for one person is slow for another. What's important is whether you wrote *fast* for you. So did you?

Silently read what you wrote. What word best describes it? Silly? Weird? Revealing? Writers have names for such fast-writes: "the bone pile" or "compost" or "river-words" or "stuff." We call ours "garbage," but we pronounce it gar-BAHZ—so people will know it's important.

You may be able to "judge" Dream-write 1 by how it looks. Does it look careless, scribbled, or typed-too-fast? Are there misspelled words? Letters left out of words, words left out of phrases? Other dumb mistakes?

Good! You're on your way to dream-write.

Step 4. (If you're working with someone else . . .) It's your partner's turn, you keeping time while he/she fast-writes. Have her/him count the words.

When it's your turn again, have your partner time you for one minute. Try to add ten words to your total. Or more. If you wrote twenty-three words in Dream-write 1, try for thirty-three in Dream-write 2. (You're numbering dream-writes so you can keep track of them.)

When your partner says GO, don't think, don't stop, don't worry about spelling or other errors. JUST WRITE FAST.

When you're finished, put the number of words in a circle at the end.

Did you add ten? If YES, smile. (If you added fifteen, GRIN.)

Step 5. Here's an example from us, written on our word processor.

Dream-Write Sample #1

i'm jst sitting, tyring to write real fast, wondering whast to say, it shjont] seem to ahve anythingk as on my mind. ywelll, there's the trip i didn t get to take, i was all set to go canoeinkg with Pete kand he had to cancel, i was all packed, wondering whether we'd freeze. tv show where some explorere was frozen in sold block fo ice. someone said there was snow in canqada and minneseora. yoi can freeze. . . . (78 words.)

Seventy-eight words per minute is very fast, for us. When we first practiced dream-write, we worried about what to say, about finding the right word, about spelling and such. At the start, we'd write 18 to 25 words by hand. By word processor or typewriter, we'd write 25 to 40.

Now, when we dream-write, we just do what we told you to—WRITE AS FAST AS WE CAN AND ACCEPT WHATEVER COMES OUR WAY.

We'll use these dream-writes later.

How did you get so good? you wonder.
Practice, man, practice.

Dream-Write 2

Introduction

To get to the point where your gar-BAHZ is truly useful as "raw material," you need to *practice* dream-writing. We're not talking ten minutes or so; we're talking *beaucoup* repetitions. You need these "reps" to become an accomplished dream-writer. You need to practice until you're free of worry about WHAT your dream-write says, or about HOW IT SAYS WHAT IT SAYS. You need to practice until you slip into dream-like writing speed, where whatever comes to you *during* and *through* the writing is OK.

If you become an accomplished dream-writer, you'll have an advantage over others. Dream-writing looks easy; fruitful dream-writing isn't. Many won't be willing to learn how to dream-write and to practice.

Do it! You might become a star!

Dream-Write Steps

Step 1.

Practice eight or so more timed dream-writes. When you feel you're ready, lengthen the time of writing to two minutes, and then to three minutes. Sometimes it takes time to get into things. Do your dream-writes one right after the other, or spread them over several days.

Number each dream-write and put the number of words at the end.

You should have dream-writes numbered 1 through 10 when you are finished.

Step 2.

In each case, *your goal is to write fast enough to become "dream-like."* It isn't easy to say what "dream-like" is. In night-time dreams, ordinary things become extra-ordinary. For example, people who have never appeared together in real life appear together in dreams. In dreams, people travel in unreal ways—floating, flying, suddenly appearing as if by magic in some new place.

It is difficult to "get that wild" through dream-write. It is difficult to leave the censor behind, and to accept whatever comes. It is also difficult *not* to worry about "making sense." But to "not making sense" is where dream-writing should take you.

How will you know when you're there?

Perhaps the best test comes from reading over your dream-writes. Are they surprising and wild? Did you catch yourself thinking, "Gosh, did I write that?" Did you feel yourself gasp (just a little) at what you wrote?

Save your dream-write practices for later use.

Step 3.   Here's our sample:

> OUtside it's darekning and swallows start to fly. Bats, small birds. I launch from the back steps and join them, tyaking a perch on the backyard fence. I try to talk but my throat is bird tight, what i want to say comes out like a caw or a corak. "good evening" or "nice weather foir flying" (1 minute. 56 words. <u>Too slow!</u>)

Interlude

Getting Out of Your Self

Are dreams real? Where do they come from? If they are not really a part of your self, why are they yours and not someone else's?

But they really are different from the waking world, where you have to be on time, obey certain regulations—and certainly obey gravity and other forces (forces that need not exist in a dream).

Somehow, we might face up to realities but still hold onto what dreaming and thought can do to "reality." Maybe that extra quirk in life is what makes artists and thinkers free.

We have to reach both directions, and that's why these exercises alternate between the flights of the self and the burdens of the surrounding world. . . .

List Poems

Introduction

Already you've practiced lists of sorts—the acrostic, with its listing of letters to start off lines; the recipe poem, with its list of ingredients and ways of combining them. And if you're like us, you've made other lists that have no connection with poetry: "People for the party," "Phone numbers," and "Things I gotta do *now!*"

But back to poems: Are there lists in everyday kinds of poems? Sure. Gary Snyder includes a list of wild foods in "Hunting":

> Mescal, yucca fruit, pinyon, acorns,
> prickly pear, sumac berry, cactus
> spurge, dropseed, lip fern, corn . . .

In her best-known sonnet, Elizabeth Barrett Browning answers her question "How do I love thee?" with "Let me count the ways":

> . . . I love thee freely, as men strive for Right;
> I love thee purely, as they turn from Praise.
> I love thee with the passion put to use
> In my old griefs, and my childhood's faith . . .

Between those two in complexity is this list from Walt Whitman's <u>Song of Myself</u>:

> I hear the bravura of birds . . . the bustle of growing
> wheat . . . gossip of flames . . . clack of sticks cooking
> my meals. . . . I hear the sound of the human voice . . . a
> voice I love. . . .

Examples like these, added to recipes and acrostics, broaden the definition of *list*. Broadly defined, list poems are common indeed.

List-Poem Steps

Here's a "list with a twist." Basically, the poem is a list of images. But at the end the poet sort of answers the "So what?" question.

Step 1.

Text 10

The Grocer's Children

The grocer's children
eat day-old bread
moldy cakes and cheese,
soft black bananas
on stale shredded wheat,
weeviled rice, their plates

heaped high with wilted
greens, bruised fruit
surprise treats
from unlabeled cans,
tainted meat.
The grocer's children
never go hungry

—Herbert Scott

Notice how items listed are made more than plain. Plain bread and bananas are made into images that are seen, tasted, smelled, and felt. Bread is <u>day-old,</u> bananas are <u>soft</u> and <u>black,</u> cakes are <u>moldy,</u> and so on.

Also notice how the last two lines are an answer of sorts to that old question, "So what?" It's as if the poem is saying, "Get it? Here's the point: 'The grocer's children / never go hungry.' See?"

And we *do* get it. Sure, they'll never go hungry, those grocer's kids. But we're reminded of what they've been given to eat. Yuck.

Adding a twist (as in "The Grocer's Children") is skating on thin ice. It's hard to do well. There are dangers. Inexperienced poets often tack comments or explanations to the ends of their poems. They want to make sure their readers "get it."

Most poems by experienced poets don't have such endings. Theirs are more like little plays: the curtain opens, the play (usually starting in the middle of things) happens, and the curtain closes. Nobody comes out afterward to explain.

Still, here's "The Grocer's Children." Does the tacked-on ending help the poem "go somewhere," after all? Maybe it's something like this: endings that explain what readers already know *for sure* may be the endings to cut.

Does the ending of "The Grocer's Children" contribute to the poem? Or, to ask it another way, do you prefer to have meanings hinted at, or pinned down? subtle or clear?

You could probably read "The Grocer's Children" without its final two lines and still get some "so what." But not all of it?

Draft a poem like "The Grocer's Children." Make your list from something other than groceries. Add an ending that gives a twist or adds meaning. You can remove the ending later if you wish.

Step 2. Notebook and pen in hand, *take a little stroll* in the outside world. Actually move through space. As you move, senses alert, jot down what you see and what's happening: Bird. Squirrel. Stone.

Notice such things and turn them into images:

(a) That blue-ish bird, pecking away.

(b) Squirrel, sitting like a beggar.

(c) That stone, smiling, shaped like a biscuit.

Here's another good way to work: jot down questions and then answer them. For example:
Who else has breathed this very air? Not Miss Monica Morris!

List <u>fifteen or more</u> items.
Then transform several of your plain items into metaphors.
METAPHORS?
You make 'em every day: Charley's a rat. Melissa's bike is a monster. Harlan horses around. Metaphors.
A metaphor says one thing ("the sun") is something else ("a tiger").
"The sun is a tiger" is a metaphor. In a poem it might become . . .

"Red-splash tiger creeps across the sky."

Transform one or more plain items from your list. Your (a) <u>bluejay</u> becomes <u>a streak of sky,</u> your (b) gray <u>squirrel</u> is <u>an acrobat, tumbling off his ladder of air,</u> that (c) dumb <u>stone</u> somehow becomes <u>mother pig, snug in afternoon sun.</u>
Some good poems begin with such metaphors:

(a) The jay, blurry thread of blue . . .

(b) Gray acrobat, sure-footing down . . .

(c) Snug as sun the stone's first-born . . .

Step 3. Draft a "trip" poem based on the events, things, and metaphors from your walk. These questions may help.

(A) Is there an item or image from your list that seems strong, even wants to "take over"? (Sometimes metaphors try this.) Should you encourage it?

(B) Would it be good to "frame" your trip-list draft? Give it a little context? Make it more story-like? For example:

> I tell my bumptious children just
> what I saw by Milamoo Marsh . . .

and Things he'd seen
and things he'd heard
sailed his head
like bats at night . . .

Even without such a frame a trip poem can deliver surprises and lifts. Here's a poem you could use as a model for your own images:

Text 11

Cache Street North

Gum wrappers with nothing, Coors can
(flat), spilled—raspberry?—ice cream,
little torn flag, incredibly smashed pine
cone, Bud bottle half full of—maybe—
beer, gravel, gravel, piece of a
sign—"meet you at M . . . "—big
baked truck tread tracks in mud
climbing the curb, and across from the giant
timbers of the Chamber of Commerce, just where
town hesitates before the swooping scene,
one tiny shard of glass, blue, so
intense it shines like the Pharaoh's eyes
in the dark when they closed his tomb.

Just an image list from a poet's evening stroll—to which
language lends its lifts: *mystery* (Is it beer in the Bud bottle? Who or
what is "M"? How does a town "hesitate"?); *surprise* (What do those
truck treads imply?); and *sound effects:* Say "big / baked truck tread
tracks" fast, three times. (What kind of *quirk* connected the Pharaoh's
eyes with Cache Street North, anyway?).

Step 4.   Some things come in set quantities. Twins, for example. String
quartets. Eggs. You'll think of others. Might you find a poem in a
set?

Say you decide to write a baseball list poem. How many items
in the list (that is, on the team)? Nine players, is one good
answer—unless you're an American League fan and want to add
Designated Hitter. Or bat boy, manager, radio announcer, fan . . .
(*Stop!* Let's keep it simple.)

How many players? Let's say nine. We'll put nine players in
our list.

What player shall we start with? (Experiment with different
players. What you finally choose will affect how the poem turns out.)

Who comes next? (Does it make any difference? Sure.)

Try to connect the player's position and the images you
choose.

Text 12

The third baseman dreams of a ball
bouncing once, swelling like an
avalanche, leaping into his glove
like a homeless needing a bed.
The second baseman sleeps on nails.
His twin children call their porcupine
"Here Knives! Here!" their hands ablaze
from handling scraps of raw meat.
When he gets home from the twi-night

doubleheader the first baseman reads
<u>Jack and the Beanstalk.</u> Spaghetti
simmers and roils. After dinner Jack
squints the northern sky for geese.
                    (From "Baseball Player List")

Jot down several sets that come in known numbers. We don't want to stifle your imagination with examples, but think both of "natural things" (the planets, eight-legged beasts) and of artificial sets (signs of the zodiac, days of the week).
Draft a poem based on the set that interests you most.

Step 5.   **In your Notebook:** *Enter a second draft of one of the three list poems* you have written for this exercise—the "list with a twist," the trip poem, or "sets."

Extra credit. *Believe in it?* You may enjoy complicating this simple idea of "sets." Apply the number of the set to the form of your poem.

For example, give one line (or one stanza) to each item in your set. A poem based on the week might be seven lines long, one line—more or less—for each day.

Or, harder to do, have the number of words in each line be the same as the number of items in your set.

Or, even harder, have the number of items in your set be the same as (a) the number of words or syllables in the title, (b) the number of lines in the poem, and (c) the number of words or syllables in each line.

WHY DO THIS?

Well, it might be fun.

Also, there may be useful tension between some arbitrary form—such as a set number of syllables per line—and language and ideas. In bringing language and form together, good results can occur. Also, it may drive you crazy.

Here's an example of "extra credit" work. We decided to use "fives" in our basketball poem. And we decided to count syllables.

Text 13   **Big Jim Dunks One Through**

The gangly center
fakes five directions
at once: stops, spins, jumps
grabs the bullet pass
jams the ball down through.

Five syllables in the title, five lines, each with five syllables. (We notice that one-syllable words—monosyllables—give us an equal number of words and syllables. As in the title. Well, that figures.)

If syllable counting seems tricky, base your form on word count. Word counts are sly: they give you most of the problems syllables do.

Poems in Response

Why Do I Hate You?

Why do I hate you?
Let me list the whys:

I hate your beauty, so much more than mine;
I hate those lips, in smiles they always shine.
I hate the radiance of those violet eyes,
And what those lashes do to all the guys.

I hate that body even when it's fat.
Though rather slim, I never look like that.
That soft, sweet voice I've grown so to detest
It fits so perfectly with all the rest.

I hate those men who fall down at your feet.
You're always listed among the most elite.
For my own grandmother, I'd gladly be the jailer
If only I could look like you, Elizabeth Taylor.

—Sister Brigid O'Donoghue

A True Refrigerator Door Story

Dear Dad,

While Mom and I are gone
please do not forget to:

feed the mice
change the frogs' water
fix my bike
water the cactus on my desk
tape The Simpsons
buy more baseball cards
take out the trash
recycle your beer cans

Love, James
Age 8

—Carol Jago

THE FAIR WORKERS

The fair workers spread
fresh, new, yellow straw
in white, wooden stalls,
pour hard, dry grain and
soft, wet silage into big,

black buckets for black
and white cows to eat,
start the gentle humming
of the milking system
and let the shiny, gray
milkers extract the pure,
white milk from the pink
udders, hose down the
animals with long, green
hoses, parade bright and
clipped Holsteins around
a grassy ring with loud,
cheering crowds all around,
and finally, rake out moldy,
old straw with strong, wooden
rakes.

—Paula Lee

Waiting

So many times
you have left me
waiting—
  by the phone
    at the window
      after work
        by the mailbox
          before dinner
            to see a show.

The reasons
were always good
as excuses go—
  last-minute assignment
    drop-in guests
      important business call
        car trouble
          weather trouble
          money.

I'm sure tonight's explanation
will make it all
seem right

again.

—Glynn Bridgewater

Before the Party

Angela, Alex, Jennifer, Heather and
    Bill.
Kathy and Erin, Jeanette and William.
        I want to invite Steven, but I don't
        know his girlfriend Hilary.
Belle and Clae don't get along and
        Curtis bores everybody.
Amy's friends with us, but no one
is really friends with her boyfriend
        Brooke's going out of town—wait!
        So is Kathy. UGGHH Scratch them.

Then there's Joe, and how about Chuck?
        Maybe Jason and Ryan
I want everyone to get along.
        I KNOW! Stacey can come—She's
        funny.
Just like my grandma always says:
A Party Planner's Prior People Planning
Prevents Poor Parties.

                            —Belle Vukovich

January starts every year,
And every year February follows.
Then comes March to end the winter.
April's clouds cry till they're hollow.

May begins the warmer months,
But it's June that makes the flowers grow.
July comes in with fireworks
That make August all aglow.

In September, the winds grow chilly,
October's leaves begin to turn.
November is a blaze of color,
But it's for December that I yearn.

                            —Amy Waller

Give Me Five

Begin with the pointer for it leads others
    when it extends itself
    and those around retreat.
The middle finger comes first to a handshake
    yet troubles its neighbors to cower
    when it stands in defiance.
The ring finger commits itself to carry circles
    that bind and glitter;
    among the fingers it is well-protected
    and has no will of its own.
The little finger both lives on the edge
    and stands out at afternoon tea.

Thumb.   Solid and squat,
    it opposes its neighbors
        across the valley.
    Alone, it pushes buttons and pulls strings,
        dictates life or death
            with its ups and downs.

Together thumb and its neighbors make
    a handsome fist   or
    beautiful music.

Give them a hand.

—Mary Moebius

WEST MILFORD, NEW JERSEY*

I always liked winter
the most
You could make snow pops
using snow right off the ground.
There were lots
of things to eat,
icicles
and clean snow
and dirty snow.
Then holiday treats,
candy canes
and fruitcake
and fudge
and lots of ice cream
and eggnog

Sipping hot cocoa
sitting by the blazing fire
and listening to
the carolers
outside
in the street
and going to
church
with your family.
Bundle up.
Wear galoshes,
and feel
the spirit
all the time,
not only when
receiving gifts.

—Heidi Wortman
(*Credit given to
Nikki Giovanni for
"Knoxville, Tennessee")

Under the Table

Under the table
live various types
of discarded commodities.
Hidden "Special K," dirty
knives, hard meat wrapped
quietly in napkins, the
old molded fat off the
fattened calf, dry
crusted buns, unwanted
stiff, cold snow peas,
overcooked green beans no
longer snapping, and blah
tasting cabbage all
loosely wrapped in paper
and tissue. They hold
their breath until dinner
is over and the dog comes
sniffing.

—Andrea Clark

Harrison Reunion

On the second Sunday of June no matter the weather
armed with heavy platter paper plates, my sisters
and I scrambled into line, shuffling right past Aunt
Dottie's Wonderbread bologna and butter sandwiches
because Mom had warned us that "She just never
could cook or do her share and don't you touch her
Jello either because little Mary mixed it and did
you see her filthy hands?" heading on straight for
Aunt Marion's macaroni and cheese—oven baked
not out of a box then making a judgment call
between two fried chickens wanting Mom's not
Doris' because her big boys had chased us that one
time, all the while skipping the canned beans
Grandma's boiled spam Vivian's store-bought salads
Billie's solitary dried-out date nut bread
leaving room for Little Russell's sweet
meatballs Gail's marshmallow fruit salad
and large scoops of mustard potato salad
but carefully saving a clean section for
Mom's sour cream devil's food cake some
old great aunt's strawberry rhubarb
crisp a stash of wet black watermelon
seed bullets and just a sliver of raisin
cream pie so Dad could snitch a bit when
we weren't looking; and even though we
had picked through and passed up plenty,
our plates were heaped because
we knew there was no going back.

                                          —Margaret Finders

Interlude

How to Be Strong

You can't go far wrong on a list. That is, you can't be wavering, or very sentimental, or just <u>empty</u> in what you write.

And did you notice that when you mention something it tends to hint at other things? And they begin to add up, those pieces of your poem; they can't help suggesting whatever associations the things have: cactus brings in desert, which brings in a tough life; glass suggests eyes; eyes suggest color. The circle of association spreads outward, and sooner or later any list begins to create a feeling, maybe a conclusion, maybe a (not mentioned) "truth."

You can pound the readers with your language, take a swing at them, or tickle them. You have so many moves to make! A whole world full of useful <u>things.</u> And all you have to do is to mention them—they'll do the rest.

Pantoums

Introduction

You know that some poems look skinny, some look fat. That some poems rhyme and/or have a regular beat, others don't. Some poems have only a few lines, others have many. Such qualities are aspects of *form*.

You remember *form*. You began working with it at the start in your found poem. You remember that the letter poem also has a form, of sorts: "Dear Wind," it begins. So with the recipe, the acrostic, and the list poem.

Still, most modern poems are mainly shaped as they are being worked on. Patterns emerge from the work. Within those poems that have a general shape, like those in our exercises, come individual patterns of sound, rhythm, and shape.

Many great poems, however, come in established patterns that have been around a long time. Ballads, sonnets, odes. When poets work with such forms, it's as much a case of filling and using the form as of developing individual patterns. Remember haiku? Remember the haiku pattern?

Remember the sonnet? Remember its fourteen lines, its da-DAH da-DAH da-DAH da-DAH da-DAH (iambic pentameter) lines?

This exercise presents the friendliest form we know. It has a firm pattern, and yet—inside that pattern—variations without end.

Read this poem aloud, unless doing that where you are would be uncool. What do you notice? What rules were followed in writing it?

Text 14

The Summer We Didn't Die

That year, that summer, that vacation
we played there in the cottonwood—
we were young; we had to be brave.
Far out on those limbs above air,

We played there in the cottonwood   (5)
above grown-ups who shouted, "Come down!"
Far out on those limbs above air
we were brave in that summer that year.

Above grownups who shouted, "Come down,
you'll be killed!" we were scared but held on.   (10)
We were brave in that summer that year.
No one could make us come down.

"You'll be killed!" We were scared, but held on.
That year, that summer, that vacation,
no one could make us come down.   (15)

We were young. We had to be brave.

If possible, discuss the form with someone. Probably the first thing that catches your eyes and ears is the repetitions: entire lines!

Pencil in hand, read the poem again. *Can you note the pattern of repeats?* Let's see: line 2 is repeated as line 5. And line 4 as line 7. Hmmm. What other lines repeat?

Now read this poem aloud. Has it the same general pattern?

Text 15   **Heckedy Peg**   (Repeated lines)

(1) Heckedy Peg lost her leg!
(2) It happened in a jerk.
(3) Oh, she's the evil-tempered hag
(4) Whose mind had gone berserk.

(5) It happened in a jerk?   Line 2
(6) Alas, there was no time to think
(7) Her mind had gone berserk   Line 4
(8) Yes! and it happened in a wink.

(9) There was no time to think   Line 6
(10) Nobody knew what to do
(11) It happened in a wink   Line 8
(12) Real gross—and bloody too!

(13) Nobody knew what to do   ?
(14) She's the evil-tempered hag.   ?
(15) It was gross—and bloody too   ?
(16) When Heckedy Peg lost her leg.   ?

—Martha Demerly

Once you create the four lines of stanza 1, stanza 2 starts "giving back" lines. The even-numbered lines of stanza 1 (lines 2 and 4) become the odd-numbered lines of stanza 2. (More or less, that is. The poet of "Heckedy Peg" takes a few liberties.) Then the new lines of stanza 2 (lines 6 and 8) become the odd-numbered lines of stanza 3.

And stanza 4 comes entirely from earlier stanzas. *Where do lines 13 and 15 come from?* (From lines 10 and 12). *And where do lines 14 and 16 come from?* (Yes, from lines 3 and 1 in stanza 1).

Basically, that's the pantoum pattern—eight "new" lines making a sixteen-line poem.

Read this next example aloud:

Text 16   **Cold**   So this
                                                            pattern is . . .

That day was cold   (1)   Repeats as line 13   **1**
When Zero came   (2)   Repeats as line 5   **2**

We held our breath	(3)	Repeats as line 16	3
Far in the North.	(4)	Repeats as line 7	4
When Zero came	(5)		2
Our hearts went still	(6)	Repeats as line 9	5
Far in the North	(7)		4
And all our years.	(8)	Repeats as line 11	6
Our hearts went still.	(9)		5
We heard all else,	(10)	Repeats as line 14	7
And all our years	(11)		6
Beat in our hearts.	(12)	Repeats as line 15	8
That day was cold.	(13)		1
We heard all else	(14)		7
Beat in our hearts.	(15)		8
We held our breath	(16)		3

The three poems above are **pantoums** (pon-TOOMS).

The pantoum form was sent us by a friend who didn't say where he got it. So we looked it up. Three "poetry" sources agree that it comes from Malaysia and is a pattern of repeated lines or rhymes. The pantoum *in written form* has been traced back to the 1400s, so it's older even than that.

"I think it was a party poem back in the old days," says our friend. "You know, volleyball, wine, and pantoums?" (We can tell he's faking it.) "Three-legged races? They had these big pantoum parties, like celebrating a marriage, say? Some guys could keep a pantoum going for hours."

Not us. We're going to use the lean-mean *sixteen-line* form.

"Form-wise," the pantoum offers the best deal in town.

You write *eight* original lines. The pantoum form "gives you" the other eight.

"Is there more to it than that?" you ask, suspiciously.

OK. Pantoums *have* been known to drive people mad! Some persons writing pantoums for the first time have gone without food, drink, or sleep as they tinkered. Fascinating, the way things fit. Depressing, the way they don't. You'll see.

Pantoum Steps

Step 1.

Doodle six or eight words and phrases. If you're stuck, skim a magazine, book or newspaper for bits that interest you. Or go back to earlier drafts of your own and borrow from yourself. Or jot down responses to these queries: who? what? where? when? why? and (possibly) how?

Step 2.

Once you get even a few interesting words, ask what they remind you of, and write that. Try to connect a couple of pieces and draft lines. Your goal is four lines. *Number lines as you work,* so you can check them against the patterns of "Cold" and the other pantoums.

Also, leave spaces between lines for easy editing.
   Four more hints:

(a) *Think of each individual line as a separate unit.* Not as a complete sentence, necessarily, but as *somehow* complete—making a kind of sense. In "The Summer We Didn't Die," some lines are complete sentences—"We played there in the cottonwood" and "We were young; we had to be brave." Other lines aren't grammatically complete but have a sense of completeness. For example, "That year, that summer, that vacation" (line 1) and "Far out on those limbs above air" (line 4).

(b) In this first draft, for now, begin each line with a capital letter.

(c) For now, leave line ends unpunctuated.

(d) Be alert as you work to messages from the poem. Is it trying to establish connections? a rhythm? Are there rhymes and echoes? Is the poem trying to form itself? (See how "Cold" developed a four-syllable line.)

Step 3.   With the first four lines done, your pantoum is well under way. In stanza 2 you begin to repeat lines. For stanzas 2 and 3, the "even-numbered lines" of the preceding stanza become the "odd-numbered lines" of the following stanza. Line 2 becomes line 5, and line 4 becomes line 7.

But line 6 is "new." (It is natural to look at line 5 when writing line 6, but also look at line 4, which will soon be there to haunt you as line 7.)

Continue through line 12, alternating "new" and repeated lines. If you get mixed up in the form, look back at "Cold," above. Witness the pantoum form driving you toward discovering new connections, new meanings—and new problems.

Step 4.   When you come to stanza 4 (lines 13 through 16), your work is almost over. All lines in stanza 4 are repeats. The pantoum form "writes" lines 13 through 16. Still, you have to decide on what order you will use.

One pantoum pattern repeats line 1 as line 16. This "rounding off" can be satisfying. So first try to end stanza 4 **by repeating line 1 as line 16.** "Heckedy Peg" does this: 10, 3, 12, and 1. (Does it work for your pantoum? Or can you, with minor adjustments, *make* it work?)

Next try the concluding pattern of "The Summer We Didn't Die": 10, 1, 12 and 3. (Is it, with whatever adjustments you can make, a better final stanza?)

Then try other sequences. Try the pattern of "Cold," with its 1, 10, 12, 3. Another pattern is 1, 3, 10, and 12. Find what seems best.

"But which pattern is right?" you wonder.

Not to worry. There isn't a "right" answer. Your last stanza must include lines 1, 3, 10, and 12. Use whatever pattern works. Relax.

Step 5. In general, the "pure pantoum" repeats the words of a line exactly, except for "allowable" changes in capitalization and punctuation. A more liberal view, *the one we take here,* is that of repeating lines *pretty much* as they first appear. Yes! So the taking of tasteful liberties is OK.

(What *exactly* do we mean?) Well, slight changes in forms of words and phrases, capitalization, punctuation, and spelling.

Here's our rule: BE PURE IN SPIRIT, BUT ALSO BE PRACTICAL.

Here's our interpretation of our rule: Make what changes you must, but . . . Don't ruin the fun by solving all problems with "exceptions."

Editing Toward a Second Draft

Tinker with this first draft to your heart's content. As you tinker, look for chances to substitute *specific* images for more general ones. (We prefer "Heckedy Peg has lost her leg!" to "A little girl has lost a limb.")

Look also for chances to rhyme—not only the "full rhymes" that dominate "Heckedy Peg." (But notice *leg* and *hag.* Say them out loud. We like the partial rhyme of *leg* and *hag* as well as the full rhyme *jerk* and *berserk,* or *think* and *wink.* Better, in fact!)

Nor need the rhymes be only at line ends. Find other places.

Look for chances to make the poem sound good—through rhythms and sounds. Read aloud frequently. Let your ear be your teacher.

We almost guarantee fun with the pantoum. We almost guarantee some weird results and satisfying surprises as your pantoum staggers along.

We said *almost.*

In your Notebook: *Copy whatever becomes your best draft.*

DESERTED HOUSE

Questions linger in the tall grass.
The clouds pile up, filling the sky
without an answer to the grass
or the last sunlight slanting low.

The clouds pile up, filling the sky
over the long abandoned house
with the last sunlight slanting low
reflected in broken windows.

Over the long abandoned house
the night birds veer and dart away
reflected in broken windows
and we are alone by the house.

The night birds veer and dart away.
Questions linger in the tall grass
and we are alone by the house
without an answer to the grass.

—Robert King

Before my sister's visit
I clean bathrooms
Shake the striped rag rugs
Vacuum the heavy Oriental carpets

I clean bathrooms
Polish furniture with wax that smells like our garage
Vacuum the Oriental carpets
Dust the dark wood floors

Polish furniture with wax that smells like our garage
Buy Sumatran coffee, shortbread, a new book or two
Dust the dark wood floors
Readying the house, knowing she will notice the imperfections

Buy Sumatran coffee, shortbread, a new book or two
Shake the rag rugs
Readying the house, hoping she can accept my imperfections
When my sister visits.

—Janet Bouldin

Loneliness

A lone bird flying south.
One star shining in the darkness.
A secret which cannot be shared.
A locked door with no key.

One star shining in the darkness.
A hollow tree, rotting.
A locked door with no key.
A single leaf upon a limb.

A hollow tree, rotting.
A baby's cry in an empty room.
A single leaf upon a limb.
The sigh of wind on an empty street.

A baby's cry in an empty room.
A dreamless slumber.
The sigh of wind on an empty street.
A lone bird flying south.

—Michael Bailey

Gambler's Reprieve

My lady, Luck, was in a rut
before tonight at Hazel Park.
But Misty Moon avoided muck
and won—despite a dreadful start—

the third, tonight at Hazel Park.
Advance Design is on the rail
and wins despite her dreadful start.
Oh Superfecta, do not fail!

Advance Design was on the rail
but swung the turn and ran for home.
Oh Superfecta, please don't fail!
A win by Splurge! Now Bound To Roam

swings around and heads for home!
Ol' Misty Moon avoided muck,
now wins by Splurge and Bound To Roam:
my lady, Luck, has come unstuck.

—William Burns

We were drinking our coffee
We sat at sticky tables
Waiters brought beignets
We were lost to ourselves

We sat at sticky tables
Wandering jazzmen played
We were lost to ourselves
While sparrows competed for our crumbs

Wandering jazzmen played
When you suddenly looked at me
While sparrows competed for our crumbs
Where before there had been nothing

Waiters brought beignets
We were drinking our coffee
When you suddenly looked at me
Where before there had been nothing

—Pamela Merideth

For Sherwood Anderson's Clara Butterworth

Clara noticed the foreman's hands—
the callouses, the earth laced fingers,
gnarled, age-roughed,
she imagines these hands against her cheek.

The callouses, the earth laced fingers,
old hands that know when sap will run.
She imagines these hands against her cheek,
Knowledge weighted and summer night gentle.

They know when sap runs,
These hands that have birthed fifty springs of colts,
Knowledge weighted and summer night gentle—
And she is a winter-dead tree, awakening.

These hands that have birthed fifty springs of colts—
gnarled, age roughed,
She is a winter-dead tree, awakening
and Clara noticed the foreman's hands.

—Kathryn Gonier

Labor

It's time to move,
Rush around no time to waste.
It's coming quickly
Let's go now!

Rush around no time to waste!
Red light or green light . . .
Go, go, go
It's getting closer!

It's coming quickly
Get inside hurry!
It's time to move.
Let's go now!

Go, go, go
It's coming, it's here!
A head, the shoulders,
Oh look at my little dear!

—Michelle Owen

Yesterday's Stars

That night by the church.
Stars smiled above, watching us fall.
Mosquitos tickled; crickets laughed.
But we didn't feel; we didn't hear.

Stars smiled above, watching us fall.
Remember how we talked in your old Buick?
But we didn't feel; we didn't hear.
That night honesty surprised me and you.

Remember how we talked in your old Buick?
I wanted to know you better than I knew myself.
That night, honesty surprised me and you.
Tonight, my eyes are playing with yesterday's stars.

That night by the church.
Mosquitos tickled; crickets laughed.
I wanted to know you better than I know myself.
Tonight, my eyes are playing with yesterday's stars.

—Jenny Jernberg

Young Bess

Never before had they seen such a one as her.
Could this be Great Harry's daughter?
She stood before them,
Light eyes watching their every move.

Could this be their Harry's daughter?
So delicate and pale,
Light eyes watching their every move,
This girl, whose mother was a witch?

So delicate and pale,
She was the lion's cub?
This girl, whose mother was a witch,
Was the daughter of a king?

She stood before them,
The daughter of a king,
The lion's cub,
And never before had they seen such a queen as her.

—Sara Weythman

The Evil Tractor of Highway Five

The bright red tractor haunts my dreams
with blinding hi-beam headlights.
Powered forward by my screams
it stops at all the yield signs.

With blinding hi-beam headlights
it burns into my sweating eyes
it stops at all the yield signs
and then the Cocker Spaniel dies.

It burns into my sweating eyes
with fiery gold and neon green
and then the cocker spaniel dies—
its corpse emerges from the steam.

Its corpse emerges from the steam
powered forward by my screams.
With fiery gold and neon green
the bright red tractor haunts my dreams.

—Kimberly Williamson

Grandpa's Old Rope Swing

I reached out to grasp a cloud.
Up high, among the treetops,
on Grandpa's old rope swing.
I held on so tight; my heart beat in my ears.

Up high, among the treetops,
the breeze whipped through my hair.
I held on so tight; my heart beat in my ears.
The world around me forgotten for a moment.

The breeze whipped through my hair,
those summers of my childhood.
The world around me forgotten for a moment
as I climbed higher and higher.

Those summers of my childhood.
I reached out to grasp the clouds
as I climbed higher and higher
On Grandpa's old rope swing.

—Erin Merz

They've Forgotten

I saw a Dead Head sticker on a Cadillac,
and touched my lovebeads to remind myself
of the 60's and what they did
so we could grow up in peace.

I touched my lovebeads to remind myself,
but the yuppies have forgotten what they did
so we could grow up in peace,
I want to remind them.

The yuppies have forgotten what they did,
it was they who fought for our lives.
I want to remind them,
but it's too late for them now.

I saw a Dead Head sticker on a Cadillac
and thought of the 60's and what they did.
It was they who fought for our lives,
but it's too late for them now.

—Michelle Warner

I just don't understand.
You say you'll call, then don't.
Are you trying to tell me something?
Is this the end, farewell, adios?

You say you'll call, then don't.
"Maybe he's busy."
Is this the end, farewell, adios,
A relationship gone sour?

"Maybe he's busy."
I'm tired of making excuses for you.
A relationship gone sour.
"I just wish you'd call."

I'm tired of making excuses for you.
Are you trying to tell me something?
A relationship gone sour.
I just don't understand.

                              —Carey Rollins

Interlude

Things Begin to Come Together

To repeat something is the simplest, most direct way to wring further meaning out of it. Did you notice that by mentioning things twice, by just going over them again in relation to something else, and by dragging earlier parts of your poem into the later parts—you accumulated power?

"Friends, Romans, Countrymen. . . ." "I came, I saw, I conquered." These pounding-onward, "Take that, and that, and that," sequences create a momentum that can help you.

And in the pantoum whole lines get repeated, get a chance to do a kind of dance of their own. The reader's mind simply has to pay attention to what it already met, and in paying attention the mind turns meanings over and over, changing them, linking them in new ways.

A poem is a system of energy within itself, a little engine. And tinkering with the engine can sometimes awaken its best performance.

Imitation 1

Introduction

We waited until now to ask this question: How do people learn?

Through direct experience. Through indirect experience—hearing about, reading, viewing. Through trial and error.

All of the above, plus other ways, plus through **imitation.** By imitating people around us we learn those "normal things" almost everyone learns—how to talk, walk, make facial expressions, sing, tell stories. When we were babies, others modeled ways to walk and talk. As we were growing up, others "socialized" us—how we played, how we dressed, how and what we ate.

The general rule seems to be: *If we liked or valued something, we copied it.*

Imitation seems even more powerful when we set out to learn skills, activities, and ways that aren't as universal as walking and talking—things like shooting hoops, tap dancing, playing cello, oil painting, and, of course, "making poetry."

But wait. In addition to wanting to be *like* others, at least in some ways, we also want to be *unlike* others, want to be unique individuals.

Each of us is in fact unique. There's nobody in the universe *exactly* like you. Whatever you do in the next few minutes will be original. Unprecedented. Nobody has ever done exactly what you will do—inhabited your exact space, breathed with your lungs, smiled with your face, moved with your body—in precisely the way you will do it.

Yet there are those great "traditions" of breathing, smiling, and moving—huge histories of each of these "original" human activities. *It's all been done zillions of times.* So although unique, *we are more "like" than unlike others,* and our own breathing and smiling and moving will be pretty much like those same activities by others. There are few if any *absolutely* original breathers.

Few absolutely original poets, either. Any one poem tends to be at least something like poems already written (and also like poems yet to come). You want to be yourself: individual, unique. But to be a good poet-self, you should "know the tradition"—some of those poems written by others.

Knowing the tradition may be a necessary first step in "developing one's own voice." Some say that you *have* to know the tradition in order to contribute your own uniqueness. Once you've learned enough from others, you'll begin putting your own twists on the tradition.

Try it. Read and copy poems of others. Memorize a couple you like. Discover what others can do that you haven't yet learned to do. Imitate tricks you haven't yet learned. Give credit whenever a "model" has taught you something.

We imitate not so much to be like someone else as *to learn what she/he has already learned. When we know enough about how a poem is made, we are free to put our own stamp on things.*

A question to begin with: What are these accomplished poets doing that I'm *not* doing? Another useful question: How can I take from others what I need, without being unethical or breaking laws?

Copying Steps

Step 1.

On a blank sheet of paper **copy** Text 17. You may substitute hand writing for type; otherwise, make your copy exact. Use the exact words of the original, the same spellings, punctuations—*everything!* Even end each line where Text 17 ends its lines—with <u>make, what, half, are,</u> *et cetera.*

Text 17

These two suggestions may help you make
perfect copies and also help you understand what
what you copied. (1) Use your free hand (or half
a sheet of paper) as a guide to the text yiou are
copying. Try that right now—marking your
place here in Text 17. (2) Sound each word
"silently" as you write it. Even width your lips
closed tight, you can "say" words so you hear
them inside your head. Try that. Close your lips
tight. Say these words "silently aloud":
          morning   silent   tamarack   see

Step 2.

Even careful copiers find surprises when they check their work. And in a couple of places in Text 17, we tried to fool you. CAREFULLY CHECK YOUR COPY against the original. (Reading aloud will help. But if possible, find someone else willing to read the original aloud as you check your copy.)

Did you leave out any words? Are there misspellings? Missing punctuation?

Did you have the word <u>what</u> at the end of line 2, and again at the start of line 3?

Did you copy line 4 exactly—including the misspelled <u>yiou</u>? Line 7, where we put "width" instead of "with"?

In the last line, did the "m" of "morning" come exactly below the space between "say" and "these" above it?

If you got Text 17 <u>exactly</u> right, *smile*. Good for you. Now, whether you made a slip or two or none, *copy* Text 18 *exactly*.

Text 18

> There are many claims made for copying—that
> that it teaches vocabulary, speling, sentence sense,
> grammar, and even style. Maybe yes, maybe no.
> (If <u>yes</u>, we consider such learnings to be bonuses.)
> Poetry is writing so carefully arranged that it
> invites the reader to pay attention. Slower than
> your mouth when you tall, than your ears when
> you listen, than your brain at almost any time,
> your pokey hand helps you do that.

Check your work carefully. You know how. Did you copy those mistakes we *meant* to make—the repetition of <u>that</u> in lines 1 and 2; <u>speling</u> (for *spelling*) in line 2; <u>tall</u> for *talk*) in line 7?

Question: Does the slow pace of copying help you remember what you read? Hmmm. Something to think about.

Step 3.   Copy Text 19 exactly.

Text 19

Upon Julia's Clothes

Whenas in silks my Julia goes,
Then, then, methinks, how sweetly flows
That liquefaction of her clothes.

Next, when I cast mine eyes and see
That brave vibration each way free,
Oh, how that glittering taketh me!

—Robert Herrick

Step 4.   When you have copied Text 19 exactly, *read it aloud*, preferably *to* someone. As you read, give a slight pause to the nonpunctuated line ends—after <u>flows</u> and <u>see.</u> Give this "half a comma" pause without lowering the pitch of your voice on the <u>Thats</u> that come after <u>flows</u> and <u>see.</u> The point is to "mark the line" with your voice as you read.

When reading your own or others' poems in class, or in public, you may prefer reading without any such pause.

But the "half a comma" way of reading line ends may lead to discoveries about "what's going on out there at the end of the line" and how important lines are in shaping poems.

Footnote...   It may seem weird being asked to **copy** in order to learn to write original poems. Listen: We wouldn't introduce copying if we weren't sure that (1) exact copying requires the copier *to pay very close attention* to the original, and that (2) plenty of great writers have "practiced writing" by copying others.

From copying (and other imitation techniques) you may learn some tricks of good writers. Knowing enough may free you to be your most original self.

What *exactly* can you get from copying good poems?

In general, *exact copying requires close reading, and close reading can lead to understanding and appreciation.* More specifically, one student says he learned "how to keep a poem moving." Another says she learned how "to end a line." Copying "a poem a day," says a workshop student, led to "fluency and confidence." Another says he learned how to pack his poems with specific images. Again, copying requires that you pay close attention; by paying attention you may come to "appreciate" the craft of other poets.

All good things to learn, we think.

Interlude

A Little Rebellion

Actually we don't very much like to copy. Our habit is to pick up what's on the page, pick it up fast and hurry on. To plod through the exact wording, to write it down, to copy even the blunders—it irks us.

The idea, though, is to get inside someone else's work, to crawl in there and find out how it feels—the sequences, the little quirks that someone has indulged. There are a million ways to sequence and interrupt and add bits to a sentence—why did someone do it just this certain way? Entering someone else's quirkiness may help us to perceive our own, understand it, and then use it or change it.

And once you get some exact copying done you can begin to verge away from it, making it more and more your own.

Imitation 2

Introduction

You have had plenty of "life experience" for writing good poems. You have plenty of feelings, too. You also have plenty of words. But most beginning writers are short on writing experience. Now writing experience is not the same thing as living experience.

You already possess some basic qualifications for writing poems that you and others might come to care about. When we work with beginning writers, anyway, we see plenty of poems rich in feeling, in experience, and in language.

But most beginning writers lack writing experience. They confront problems like these:

(1) They're unsure about how to put a poem together.

(2) Many don't know where to end lines.

(3) Some believe that "real poetry" needs a special vocabulary of high-sounding, "poetic" language.

(4) Some prefer abstract images ("my loneliness, like tumbling through voids") to concrete images ("sitting inside, reading Abby on how to write Thank You's, kids rough-housing in the maple leaves outside.")

What does the beginning poet need *most* in order to achieve maximum satisfaction out of the process of writing? Hard to say. But it's probably <u>not</u> words, <u>nor</u> life experiences, <u>nor</u> personal feelings. Even beginners have enough of those.

Maybe what's needed is "a poetic way" of looking at the world. An angle of vision. *Is it impossible to learn that path to satisfaction?*

Surprisingly, you may approach it by studying the structure of poems, and how lines end, and what concrete images made of ordinary language can do for writing.

Perhaps in noting <u>ordinary language</u> here we short-change language—its specialness and richness, the histories of individual words, their connotations and ambiguities, their shifting meanings and uses. *Maybe.* (Still, we feel sure that reading good poems closely, *experiencing* how they are put together, is what most beginning poets need to do.)

Copy-change is a good way to practice. With copy-change you go beyond what can be learned from copying. You can experience how to structure poems, end lines, and work with specific images. In **Imitation 2** we ask you to imitate an experienced poet's poem and then ask that you "thank" that poet for what you have learned.

Copy-Change Steps

Text 20

Here's a sentence to imitate:

> The neighborhood's neatness occurs automatically, once the garbage collectors empty the dumpsters, and the stray dogs and raccoons have retreated from contact with humans. (24 words)

Step 1.

We'll plug in different words in imitating "the structure" of Text 20. The structure goes something like "This situation ["The neighborhood's neatness"] comes about this way ["occurs automatically"] once A and B take place."
We'll also try to use the same number of words.

> The crowd's roar softens dramatically, once the musicians wander onto the stage and the engineer starts testing his tangle of microphones and speakers. (Imitation of Text 20. 23 words.)

Copy-change Text 20 into a sentence of your own, using as few or as many words from Text 20 as you wish. Stay close to the structure of the original. In the same position that it occurs in the original, include the word <u>once</u> in your copy-change. Also, use approximately the same number of words. At the end of your sentence, give credit with a line something like this:

A copy-change of Text 20 by _____

Step 2.

In our copy-change of Text 20, we borrowed the word <u>once</u> from the original. Probably you did too. Notice this about copy-change: the words you "borrow" are often little structure-setting words like "once"—"since," "before," "first," "then," "only," and "because"—"function" words that shape the sentence's meaning. Now here's another model sentence:

Text 21

> With the first dips in August's temperatures, before the hardwoods' colors soften, mallards, canvasbacks and other species of ducks gather in "families" and rehearse for their migration to the sloughs and waterways in the south. (35 words)

We want to insert different words into the "structure" of Text 21. We'll borrow the word <u>with</u>, and the word <u>before</u>, and for our "subject" we'll imitate the one in the model—substitutes for "mallards, canvasbacks, and other species . . ." Then we'll imitate the verbs, <u>gather</u> and <u>rehearse</u>. Here's our effort:

> With apologies to no one, before the last bell rings, a stir of serious students, sweethearts, straw-haired cheerleaders, and a few male adolescent thugs put away their contraband and

gravitate toward the twin doorways of Clark High. (Imitation of Text 21. 37 words.)

Copy-change Text 21. In "the right places," use the words "with" and "before." As subjects, make a list of three or four items (similar to "mallards, canvasbacks and other ducks") and use the two verbs (as "gather" and "rehearse" in the original.) Try for 35 or so words.

Step 3.   The following poem has a structure worth learning.

Text 22   **Passing Remark**

In scenery I like flat country.
In life I don't like much to happen.

In personalities I like mild colorless people.
And in colors I prefer gray and brown.

My wife, a vivid girl from the mountains,
says, "Then why did you choose me?"

Mildly I lower my brown eyes—
there are so many things admirable people do not understand.

                                                    —William Stafford

Copy-change Text 22, imitating its structure and lines. Notice how each pair of lines (each "couplet") seems complete. Start your copy-change with the word "In" (or with some word or phrase that works the same way—e.g. "**on** coffee tables," "**inside** my pockets" or "**near** my eyes"; or such phrases as "when it comes to" or "thinking about").

Try for four or five "couplets." Have your final couplet "shift" into an action/reflection that's happening "right now." Imitate that long "explanatory" last line, too.

When you have a draft you like, *credit the poet* with something like:

"In the style of William Stafford"
(or) "After Stafford's 'Passing Remark'"

Step 4.   Read these three poems, noting in each one specifics you could imitate if you chose to.

Text 23   **Fog**

The fog comes
on little cat feet.
It sits looking
over harbor and city
on silent haunches
and then moves on.

          —Carl Sandburg

Text 24   **Magic Story for Falling Asleep**

When the last giant came out of his cave
and his bones turned into the mountain
and his clothes turned into the flowers,
nothing was left but his tooth
which my dad took home in his truck
which my granddad carved into a bed

which my mom tucks me into at night
when I dream of the last giant
when I fall asleep on the mountain.

—Nancy Willard

Text 25   **Taking the Hands**

Taking the hands of someone you love
You see they are delicate cages . . .
Tiny birds are singing
In the secluded prairies,
And in the deep valleys of the hands.

—Robert Bly

Step 5.   *Make a fast, first-draft copy-change* of Texts 23, 24, and 25, borrowing words as needed and imitating specific aspects. *Hang closely around* each model's structure. For example, imitating "Fog," you might start by wondering, "What comes how?"

[The fog comes   Rain drops
on little cat feet]   on silver wires. . . .

Give credit for each copy-change, including the title of the model poem, the author, or both.

Step 6.   Read the first-drafts aloud. Reading aloud *to others* might help you read carefully and hear what you've accomplished.
Decide which one of the three copy-changes you're most willing to carry into additional drafts. Keep the model in front of you as you work. *Give credit to the original on each draft,* even if your copy-changes range far from the original. Giving credit to the poets of the models is a way of saying, "Hey, dude! I'm trying to learn this poetry thing too."

Interlude

Some Tricky Considerations

In language, what is <u>original</u>? You learn to talk by imitating. Your sentences can't be entirely different from other people's. We all learn from each other.

And then you change things in what you say, following impulses that come to you as you go along. What you communicate is in those little changes: if your language is too outlandish people can't follow you, and if it's too ordinary they will get bored and not learn anything new.

The exercises along about here are flirting with these considerations, not to cheat by writing just like someone else, but just to find that area of originality that is yours. Close reading and then freedom—that's the idea.

Memory Map 1

Introduction

Here's a hard question: *Where do poems come from?*

You might answer, "From these exercises of yours." OK, OK.

But poems you wrote *before* you met us: where did they come from?

From the same sources as ours, we'll bet. Sometimes from something we *heard*—spoken words, sounds from the world outside, music. Sometimes from some scene we *saw*—tenderness between two people, a wild moment in nature, something beautiful or weird. Sometimes from other sensory experience—the *touch* of a patch of concrete shadowed from sun, the *smell* of rhubarb pie, the *taste* of a foggy fall day.

Such experiences remind us of other things. Some poems of ours seem to be messages. Not big messages, such as WAR IS STUPID—although it is. Little messages: I planted some onions yesterday and want to tell you how the dirt felt. (Or) I saw clouds doing something to the sky that reminded me of an afternoon in a Denver park. (Or) You're wearing the same blue shirt you wore on your birthday.

Just messages from our life. *Remembered things*, mainly. Things that stick in our minds like burrs. Odd and quirky things that interest us.

And poems come from yet other places. From remembered dreams. From reading. From images that float inexplicably into mind. Some poems start with a strong feeling, like love or fear or hope. We have a strong feeling, and it seems as if a poem might be a good way to express it.

We said it was a hard question. Poems seem to come from everywhere. If you've written poems other than our exercise poems, take time to think about how they began.

For us, many poems, probably most, start with *sensuous images*—images from the senses, that is. These connect with our experience, *with things we remember.* Wouldn't it be fine to have a dependable technique for remembering? Why you could practice writing poems any old time!

Lucky you. *Remembering* is exactly what this exercise is about.

Memory-Mapping Steps

<u>Caution:</u> Some people don't enjoy remembering back. Maybe in their younger lives bad events occurred, or persons were cruel. If your memories are too painful, you could skip "memory mapping" and go to the next exercise. But if you do, take time in the next few weeks to write toward those painful memories—not to make a poem, necessarily; more to identify and consider important issues in your life. We believe that writing even about painful things can be helpful.

Step 1. Imagine yourself standing outside the place you live now. What shape is it? What color? Try to locate the window(s) and door(s). Does anything grow out in front—grass, trees, vines? Draw a mental picture that shows the shape and color and size of where you live. Imagine yourself entering that place—noticing your hair, the look on your face, your clothes. How do you get to the place where you sleep? Up stairs? Down a hallway? Through another room? Notice people, furniture, and other rooms as you enter and walk to where you sleep.

Did you live in the same place when you were four or five or six? If YES, imagine yourself as you were. See yourself entering that place. Dress yourself in clothes you wore. Are you alone? How was the house different? Did you sleep in the same room? Imagine yourself entering and going to the room where you slept.

If you lived in a different place when you were four or five, imagine yourself standing outside *that* place. See your hair, the look on your face, your clothes. Try to get that place in mind—how it looked inside and out. Remember your route from where you entered to where you slept.

If you forget an essential detail or two, it's all right to make it up.

Step 2. On a fresh sheet of paper, draw a map (or floor plan) of the room you slept in at age four or five. Whether you slept alone, with someone else, or with a slew of people, for this exercise, think of it as *your* room.

Make your floor plan as if you are looking down on your room from the ceiling, a bird's-eye view. Fill at least half a page with your floor plan. Start with the walls, the windows, and the door or entry. If there is a closet, put that in; indicate stairs, hallways, or porches. Then put in major pieces of furniture—bed, rug, dresser, table, chair, bookshelf.

If you can't remember that room *at all*, draw your map for the first sleeping place you do remember. But really, almost surely, *you'll remember back to that younger life if you'll relax. Give yourself time.*

If you draw as badly as we do, it will be wise to *label things so they'll be clear to others.*

Check out our map on the next page—labels and all. Without labels, you wouldn't know our bed from our toy box.

When your map's done, show it to someone. If Someone seems friendly, show your map, describing your room and some things in it. Talk in the *present tense*, as if you were younger and actually back there in your room. (For example, "Chris and I sleep in this double bunk here. Me on top. Here's where I keep my frog.")

Step 3. Now we want you to add other stuff to your map. "OK," you say, "but what stuff?"

Check the ideas in **Item List** below. Questions are asked as if you are back at an earlier age and there in your sleeping room with your things where you can see them. Answer as if you are there.

Item List (MEMORY ITEMS)

(a) Where do you keep books, magazines? Name one book you love.
Sample: (a) *I keep* Curious George *under my bed where Mary won't take it.*

(b) Where do you hide secret things, contraband?
Sample: (b) *My frog skeleton stinks and Ma keeps saying, "Get rid of it."*

(c) Where's your gerbil/goldfish/turtle?

(d) Are there paintings? Other things hanging on the walls?

(e) Have you board games—ones you play? Ones you don't like? Why?

(f) Where do you collect marbles, dolls, soldiers, junk, cards, stamps. . . ?

(g) What one piece of clothing do you wear most?

(h) Where's your favorite plaything (toy)?

(i) Have you hidden money—real or make-believe? In what?

(j) Which piece of furniture do you love (or hate)?

(k) Tell about these photographs (pictures)? (Where taken? By whom?)

(l) Where'd you get that special lamp (lighting fixture, heater, clock, tool)?

(m) May I hear that instrument ("noise maker," toy, radio, phono)?

(IMAGINATION ITEMS)

(n) What do you see, looking out the window of your room? Who/What is out there? What's beyond what you can *actually* see?
Sample: *I see the fire escape up to Gorski's apartment . . .*

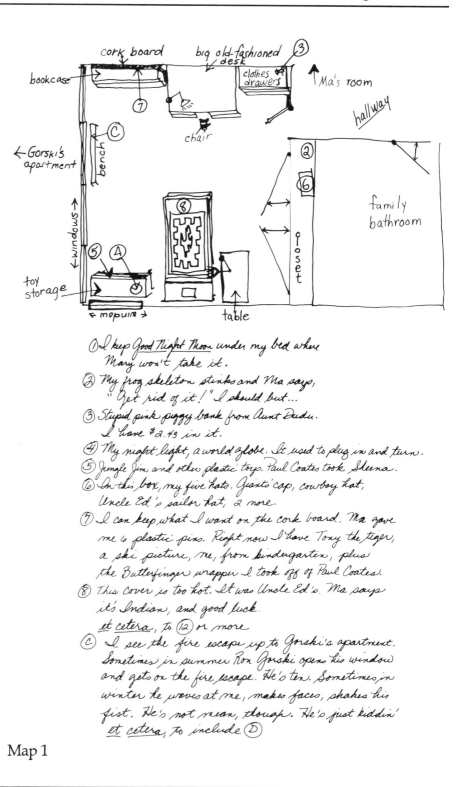

① I keep *Good Night Moon* under my bed where
   Mary won't take it.
② My frog skeleton stinks and Ma says,
   "Get rid of it!" I should but...
③ Stupid pink piggy bank from Aunt Dudu.
   I have $2.43 in it.
④ My night light, a world globe. It used to plug in and turn.
⑤ Jungle Jim and other plastic toys. Paul Coates took *Sheena*.
⑥ In this box, my five hats. Giants' cap, cowboy hat,
   Uncle Ed's sailor hat, 2 more.
⑦ I can keep what I want on the cork board. Ma gave
   me 6 plastic pins. Right now I have Tony the tiger,
   a ski picture, me, from kindergarten, plus
   the Butterfinger wrapper I took off of Paul Coates.
⑧ This cover is too hot. It was Uncle Ed's. Ma says
   it's Indian, and good luck.
   et cetera, to ⑫ or more
Ⓒ I see the fire escape up to Gorski's apartment.
   Sometimes in summer Ron Gorski opens his window
   and gets on the fire escape. He's ten. Sometimes in
   winter he waves at me, makes faces, shakes his
   fist. He's not mean, though. He's just kiddin'
   et cetera, to include Ⓓ

Map 1

(o) Where's the scary place in your room? Who/What's in that scary place? How do you make it go away?
Sample: *This big spotted snake lives on the shelf in my closet. . . .*

(p) You're playing some kind of game with a real or imaginary friend. What game? Who's playing? Who "wins" or "loses"?
Sample: *I'm on the floor playing Chinese checkers with Robert. If I don't watch, Robert will move my marbles . . .*

(q) Tomorrow's "show and tell" at school. You're supposed to bring something from your room. What will you take? Why?

(r) You've been sent to your room for being bad. Where do you go when you're feeling mad or sad? What are your feelings?

(s) You're talking with some toy. What do you say first? What does the toy say back? (Maybe write the conversation as a little script.)

Step 4.   *Write up ten or more items.* Put down the letter of the item you're writing about and jot down a few details. Writing in present tense, describe "the thing" and how it connects with your life. What's its story?
Among your ten-plus items, choose one or more from (n) thru (s).
Add *remembered* or *imagined* items of your own. Ask others to describe good items they thought up, and share your own.

(t)

(u)

(v)

et cetera

When you've written up ten or more, put the letter of each item where it belongs on your map.

Step 5.   Once your list is finished and the letters of the items are on your map, *asterisk 3–5 items that interest you most.*
Then, still in the present tense—as if you are four or five years old, as if you are there in your room, and as if what you're telling about is there with you—tell more about each asterisked item: ideas that associate with those things, feelings about them, imaginings . . . a few lines, a few sentences, maybe a paragraph.

Step 6.   These longer chunks of present-tense writings are the basis of your memory map draft. Reread them. Does a common thread run through them—an emotion (such as nostalgia) or an attitude (such as amusement)? Make a working title of any such "thread" and use it as a focusing device, e.g., "Still Mad at Sister" "Monsters" and "Little Boy Blue."

If you're already forming ideas on how you might work your chunks into a three-stanza (+) poem, draft away. More likely, the focus and title will emerge as you work. Here's a way to proceed:

(a)   Select a strong chunk as raw material for stanza 1. Start stanza 1 with words like these:
I am in my room, _____ing . . ."
Fill in a strong word that comes out of the chunk you chose. For example: "I am in my room, **peering** into Gorski's window" or "I am in my room, **praying** that the boa . . ."
Moving toward poetry, put pressure on your language. Use fewer words, and choose them carefully. Substitute specifics for general words.

(b)   Stanza 2 starts with the words below and brings in several chunks.
"Now I'm _____ing . . ."
Find a strong word for the blank. Combine chunks quickly.
E.g.,   Now I'm **covering** <u>Good Night Moon</u>
                With my pj's, hoping the snake gets loose
                When Mary is here, even though Ma
                Told her, "Stay out of T's room! . . ."

(c)   Stanza 3 uses the material from some chunk(s) you haven't already used. Stanza 3 is "happening" right now. Have the persona (or "I" character) reflect or look back on that earlier time. Start with words like
                I realize that back then . . .
(or)   **Now I see how . . .**
(or)   **Remembering, now, it's clear . . .**

You'll find ways to make the last stanza "pull together" disconnections in earlier stanzas and "explain" loose ends. However insignificant or unrelated the material of this stanza seems at first, try to make it unify (connect, comment on, explain) all the rest. But not explain *too* much, we hope. It may help to think of "I" as a character in a story or play more than as you yourself.

Step 7.   Write one more draft of your work, making whatever radical changes you wish. Should the poem begin with a different stanza? Start "later" than it now does? *Is there an unused piece from your Item List that your poem needs now?* Is it time to drop those beginnings—"I am in my room, _____ing," and the others?
You moved from "visualized" <u>raw material</u> to <u>a draft</u> to <u>revision.</u> But maybe some of the sparkle of your work got lost in the process. If so, go back to early drafts and reclaim whatever you want.
Finally, think about the physical shape this memory map poem wants to take. How do you "measure" lines? Does the poem

want to be in short lines? Long lines? Some mix of the two? Is the pattern you find for stanza 1 something to maintain in stanzas 2 and 3? Has another stanza a pattern the others should follow?

Step 8.   **In your Notebook:** *copy in a good draft of your poem from Memory Map 1.* Maybe also write your feelings about doing memory writing.

We'd guess that your map work reminded you of rich things. Are there items left over you could use for another poem?

You can add to your map as you remember more things. And you can make different maps. Any good ideas?

Why, this could go on forever!

Here's a poem we lifted from our map.

Text 26   **Third Street**

They are watching me die. Six years old
and I'm dying. "Dip-theria," they call it, and my throat
won't open, and the doctor with a look at my mother
shaking his head, then the long needle stabbing
my back, my dog Buster whining, Peggy
holding her doll and crying. Shadows lengthen
and reach up the wall. They jump. They are watching me die.

Now in the strange room of my head my shadow
escapes and floats away, leaving our street
and the vinegar factory, on past the Santa Fe tracks
and fluttery lights, over the diminishing river.
How sad that Buster on his little rug will sleep
alone, that Peggy's doll will stare button eyes
all night at my pillow, my empty bed.

If only my father could hold me forever, and the world
stay still—my little blue shirt, my elkhide shoes
waiting for Buster and me to explore Alaska
and all those ranges. . . . I see our clean walls, and the sparrow
I killed with my slingshot (how it held out its wings and fell
trembling into the dust). I will live. The doctor's
black bag will save me. His long needle will stab
again into my back and Buster will howl.

My father's eyes—I see them yearn me toward him
and carry me drifting and weak into my bed in the room.
Years later my son will die and that look
will return. Something will break in the sky that was welded
and forged back home by a thousand pledges of truth.
Third Street, I hold you here, and my throat will open.

Poems in Response

The Darkness

It's so dark
and
My fists are clenched
and
I'm sitting upright in bed,
watching the window above my bookshelf,
It's open
and
a sliver of light slices
the darkness
and
the pale, white curtains blow in
I know the spirits have come.

Quickly I turn my face away
and
when I squint through
the darkness
at the closet door
(oh)
I hope that the brassy doorknob
won't turn from
inside.

Sometimes, even now, my body
tenses up on those windy nights in
the darkness
in my new room
and
the closet doesn't have a doorknob
so
I always watch the curtains,
never knowing if
I am ever
truly
            alone.

                        —Danielle A. Durkin

Hayti, Missouri 1959

Outside the room,
an old man rocked all day on his porch.
Miss Cora had purple-blue skin;
a bent, broken Negro man cut her lawn.
Mother and Dad drank in angry silence.
Girls in tight jeans blew smoke rings
in the last booth at the drug store.
Boys tried to put their hands
under blouses in the back seats of cars.

Inside the room,
Errol Flynn rescued me from sultans,
pirates and evil plantation owners.
Carefully spaced charcoal drawn eyes
stared from a sketch pad.
I travelled to Atlanta, Spain and Russia
in books hidden under the bed.
The Virgin Mary watched from the wall,
palms and fingertips placed together.

Mornings hung like wet wool
on backyard clotheslines.
Days stretched from here to there
in ribbons of sunlight and shadows.
Plastic curtains waved in windows—
attic fans whirred and
hummed with importance.
Secrets lived in houses on streets
shaded in dust and decay.

—Lynne Dozier

There

I saw a picture of There.
There had yellow walls
and a white canopied bed
and There was once my brother's
nursery.

My bears crouched like nightmares
in their heaps and huddles,
clouding the pale thin canopy sky
with their shadows.

There had wallpaper on one wall—
brightly crayoned Holly Hobbies
who had no shoulders,
and their colors were drawn
a little outside the lines.

I remember one night
when my eyes got stuck open
so, sleepless, I snuck my light on
and stayed up very late
drawing shoulders on those poor
dolls.

—Krista Wark

window sitter

from my little blue room I look down at the ground
which isn't so far away as I chew on the window sill
and feel my insides grow hot and black as the tar
that melts in shiny rivulets in the parking lot

I watch grimy children with spindly legs chase
after the ice truck and catch splinters of ice
embedded with grit which scratches their tongues
as they suck on their fire-cold treasures
and then they are gone but not far

my forehead is branded with smudged tic-tac-toes
from the screen which bulges and is beginning
to fray but still holds me in and my eyes start to smear
'till I can't see the building where Nancy lives
though it's really not that far

I smell hot needles of spruce which dry crisp in the sun
and are no longer blue in a yard with no grass
but some butter-and-eggs with dusty skirts grow
underneath the spirea bush put there by my father
who now mows tough yellow Texas lawns and writes
long letters from too far away.

—Bonnie Jean Cousineau

Resisting the Poetry Assignment

This house is square and white and fine—
Camellias and azaleas announce the yard.
Evenings, I enter the high heavy door,
pass through a bird-papered hall;
the grandfather clock strikes five.

I don't want to go back. That house
was dark—my mother a solitary light
moving from room to room. No,
it has been too much trouble
getting from there to here, and

none of those rooms, furnished
with found things, chairs that washed up
in storms, rickety dressers with drawers
that slid easily neither out
nor in, mattered. But

there was a bookcase. With books—
Paradise Lost in a bright blue cover,
The Complete Works of Shakespeare with
real gold on the spine, and Mama's big
biology book—the one I sat and tore,
the only time I ever saw her cry.

—Anne McCrary Sullivan

In My Smaller Self

Reaching out the window
I sing to a star-paved street
Not sleeping
Not awake
In my Smaller Self.

Hearing the garden's fluorescent light
Devour a night of insects below—
Across the way the music goes,
And drunken farewells light the air
Because the moon hides in trees.

I run my fingers
Along the tops of Green Summer Shoes
I wore today
Will wear tomorrow
Until Someday, they forget to fit.

I held my breath
Because the air was so still, after,
When I wasn't sleeping
I wasn't awake
In my Smaller Self.

                    —Meghan Rosenstein

Interlude

Gold Country

When you mine your memories, many serious possibilities line up, waiting to get into your writing. Don't avoid anything, we say: reach into pain or elation; turn it over and bring it back. You can use that past; you can re-live, and do it better this time.

Yes, your imagination can take part—but what is imagination? Isn't it linked right on back into your inner self? No? Then how come it occurs in different ways to different people? Your imagination is part of you, part of all those things that happened.

And when you do that visual mapping, you identify the actual objects in your life; your writing touches the real, takes on the power of those looming shapes you had to meet where you lived.

So powerful and attractive are these memories that we must break away again from the literal. Our plan is to push outward again, turning to others' words and thoughts in order to be enriched by as wide a set of experiences as possible.

The methods that follow may not be as comfortable as using your own memory and imagination, but we want you to encounter other people's peculiarities, to feel new identities that can add to your life.

Question/Answer Poems

Introduction

Who's on first? *What* do you call that doodad? *Where's* Mimi? *When* is Vic getting home? *Why* is that little red light on? *How* do we fix it? **Questions** are pretty useful out there in "the real world." Questions help us socialize. For example, two strangers are in the park, one of them lost:

> "Hey, how're you doin'?" the lost one says.
> "Oh fine, thanks. How you doin'?"
> "Actually, I'm a little lost. Do you know where the turtle pond is?"
> "Sure, that's easy. See that little gray tower there . . . ?"

Not incidentally, there's a strong (poem-like) impulse to explain unknown things in terms of something known:

> "You say you were hit in the ankle by a twanker, Miss? What exactly is a twanker?"
> "You know, a twanker. Like a bread-box on roller-skate wheels?"

Now you think we're going to say that questions and answers work in poems too. That they get things under way swiftly, provide voices, invite good details—lots of good stuff. Right again!

Question/ Answer Steps

Step 1.

A first kind of Q/A poem gives **yes/no** answers to longish questions.

> "Girl, return my beads?"
> "No."
> "You know they're mine?"
> "Yes."
> "Then hand them over?"
> "No."

Simple enough: Questions answered "yes" and "no." Here's another example. During our good old days, at parties, one person might actually ask another person to dance. That's the scene of this next **Yes/No** poem.

Text 27
May I please have this dance?
  No.
May I please have that dance?
  No.
Aren't you going to wear anything to the dance?
  Yes.
Are you a good dancer?
  Yes.
Do you know how to dance?
  No.
May I in that case have your company during the dance
they decide to play exactly at midnight, whatever it is? I
have fallen in love with your eyes, lips, hands, and hair.
  No.

—Michael Benedikt

To draft a **Yes/No** poem, think up a scene with two speakers—an older person asking a little boy if he's lost; a census-taker at the front door; a willow branch asking several finches to vamoose. *Draft four or more questions* answerable with Yes, No, or similar words. Before completing your draft, read Text 28 aloud, listening for the effects of *word spacing* and *typography*.

Text 28
Maybe

Hey Babe, love me?
        Yeah.
You know, like I love you?
              I guess.
Like we're together, I'm talkin lifetime?
                    Yeah.
Babe, somethin buggin you?
YESSss.

See if your poem might benefit from experiments with the placement of answers and with print. Mainly use Yes and No answers (or variants thereof). But if it seems a good idea, allow yourself *one* Maybe.

Step 2.   A second kind of **Q/A** asks for **names** from the answerer(s).

Text 29
Whose eyes wash with tears
each New Year's Eve?
  Father's.

Whose lies make me laugh
And stay longer at the table?
  Sam's. My baby brother Sam's.

Who used to dance her fingers
through mashed potatoes and gravy?
  Jennifer's fingers remember.

All answers are names, or "name substitutes" (e.g., "*Jennifer's fingers remember*").

To a question such as "Who's that on the diving board?" one answer might be the name "Spence." But "name substitutes" for "Spence" might work, too. (Who's that on the diving board?) *My big bro.* Or *That gorgeous hunk.* Or *One who breaks his mama's heart.*

In Text 30, note the effect of the "name substitute" in the last line.

Text 30

> Who challenged my soldier mother?
> > Nobody.
> Who kept house for her and fended off the world?
> > My father.
> Who suffered most from her oppressions?
> > My sister.
> Who became bitter when the world wouldn't listen?
> > My sister.
> Who challenged my soldier sister?
> > Nobody.
> Who grew up and saw all this and recorded it and
> kept wondering how to solve it but couldn't?
> > Guess who.

Draft a poem of four or five questions needing names or "name substitutes."

Step 3. The "5-W" poem usually gives longish answers to short questions. **"5-W"** reminds us of our days as high school newspaper reporters. Cub reporters were told to get the "five **w**'s" into their stories.

The five **w**'s? who, what, where, when, and why. (Sometimes we added an **h,** for "how").

Here's the **"5-W"** (+ **h**) as a poem. (The questions are in parentheses.)

Text 31

> **Coincidence**
>
> (who?)   Our elected representative, Ms. Ludlaw
> (what?)   pumping voters' hands
> (how?)   as if they were slot-machine levers
> (where?)   outside Faculty Lounge
> (when?)   Tuesday, after school.
> (why?)   Next month, election.

Use the question words in any order you wish. Leave out one of the question words (especially *why*) if it seems to tell too much. ("Coincidence," above, might be better off without the *why*. "September," below, seems better with it.)

Text 32

September

(what?)	Flocking toward Mexico
(when?)	before Winter's first ka-choooo,
(how?)	thrashing the silver air
(where?)	in Ontario's gray sky,
(why?)	wanting warm—
(who?)	a blizzard of ducks

Ready to write? Rehearse the **"5-W"** form. Think of someone who makes you mad, or someone who makes you laugh. Think of a place that scares you, or a place where you'd like to be. Think of a time you wished you lived in, or a time you wish you could forget. Think of the clock on the wall or a friend's cool bracelet.

Doodle out two or three **"5-W"** poems, adding **how**'s and titles if you wish. What you doodle may not change the course of Western civilization, but . . . Hey, who knows? Work until you get one you're willing to read aloud to a friend. Or to a tree.

Step 4. Probably, while drafting **"5-W"** poems you found **why** and **how** hardest to answer. For how and why questions, answers aren't so simple. A **fourth** kind of **Q/A** poem begins with a "rhetorical" question (often a why or how). A rhetorical question doesn't really expect an answer. The asker answers her/himself:

> How do I love thee?
> (or)   Why did I put the artichokes and blue goats in my bed?

If you had asked either question, you'd expect to provide your own answer. So it is with Elizabeth Barrett Browning's most famous sonnet. "How do I love thee?" the poem begins. "Thee" doesn't answer. Nor do we expect an answer from her or him. The *asker* answers. (How do I love thee?)

> Let me count the ways.
> I love thee to the depth and breadth and height
> My soul can reach, . . .

Another example of a question about to be answered by the asker is the Shakespeare sonnet that begins, "Shall I compare thee to a summer's day?" (The speaker is wondering, Is that a cool idea? Shall I do it? OK, good.)

> Thou art more lovely and more temperate . . .

In the Browning and Shakespeare poems, there's another character—a "thee/thou"—who is addressed, but never replies. Here are two clear examples where "a silent listener" is being "talked to":

> Ocean, have you mermaids,
> gems and chests of gold
> deep in your belly?

(and)   How come you made me so handsome, Sweet Jesus?

Obviously, *Ocean* and *Sweet Jesus* are addressed, or "spoken to."

Other times, it seems to be the "reader" who is addressed. The poet may pose a question only he or she *can* answer: These beginnings show "the reader" being addressed:

> Are they impatient, your little ones?

(and)   Why would anyone give a hand
to the frightful riders of night?

Still others, the speaker seems to address him- or herself. "Why did I put the artichokes and blue goats in my bed?" (Only the asker knows.) "Well, Max left the kitchen door open and I had artichokes boiling. . . ." There's no obvious "listener" in the poem. The point is, decide early whether or not to put a listener inside your poem.

Then *draft a poem that begins with a* (so-called) *rhetorical question*—maybe with **how** or **why.** You might as well ask a question you'd really like to ask, one you'd like to answer. You're the "I" in the poem—asking some big question so you can answer it.

Then, when finished with your draft, try this: *Read it aloud* **with** *and then* **without** *the rhetorical question that began it.* Which way is better? And if it's better *without,* can you find a good title in the question you've just removed?

Step 5.   **In your Notebook:** From first drafts of (1) the **Yes/No** poem, (2) the **names** poem, (3) the **"5-W,"** and (4) the **rhetorical Q,** *choose your favorite.* EXPERIMENTING with things mentioned here—type, placement of responses, name substitutes, removing the question from the poem, and *as always* with language and form—*write a second draft of one.*

Poems in Response

PERSONHOOD
  by THE QUESTIONPERSON

          AT 3 YEARS

Do you want to be President some day?   Boy. **YES**. Girl. **YES**.
Do you think you'll be married before
    you're 25?   Boy. **NO**. Girl. **YES**.
Which is easiest for you to do—build,
    buy, or play house?   Boy. **BUILD**. Girl. **PLAY**.
Are you happy?   Boy. **YES**. Girl. **YES**.

          AT 23 YEARS

Do you want to be President some day?   Man. **YES**. Woman. **NO**.
Do you think you'll be married before
    you're 25?   Man. **NO**. Woman. **NO**.
Which is easiest for you to do—build,
    buy, or play house?   Man. **BUY**. Woman. **PLAY**.
Are you happy?   Man. **YES**. Woman. **NO**.

                              —Karen N. Reynolds

First Day Back at School

What did you do this summer?
    Nothing
You didn't go anywhere?
    No.
How come?
    I don't know.
You must have done something?
    Not really.
You stayed in your house all summer and did nothing?
    I went to K-Mart a lot!
Ha! Is that all?
    No.
What else?
    All summer I dreaded you asking me what I did!

                              —Jennifer Plunk

Can I reach to the stars
Yes
And not be called too small

Can I tell the world my dream
Yes
And not be called bizarre

Can my tiny finger point at a universe,
    imploring them to see

Yes

And if you reach
                    and tell
                                and point

You'll be called a fool
                    like me.

—Christine Kolaya

Just Another Day

Who left the water running?
    Justin knows.
Whose crying kept me up all night?
    Kristian cries all the time.
Who kicked Justin in the stomach?
    I saw Dan—he did it!
Whose diaper needs to be changed?
    Kassy—phew!
Who threw up on this brand new shirt?
    The shy one from across the street.
Whose love and patience will fix everything?
    Yours truly.

—Sadie Tirmizi

Family Therapy

Who has a body like a cage of pain?
    Mother
Who buried his parents before he memorized their faces?
    Father
Who never quit the war and regiment?
    Son
Who has dreams more real than sweethearts?
    Daughter
Where do they keep their secrets?
    The jails of their eyes
What are all the wrong reasons?
    Dignity, Shame, Remorse
What strips them clean?
    Screams like spears
Who shows them home another way?
    Strangers

—Lahna Diskin

Who's the free spirited traveler
with all the mileage?
    The wanderer—Shelley

Who's the responsible one
with the balanced checkbook?
    The saver—Margaret

Who's the goofy and silly one
with that permanent smile?
    The clown—Michelle

Who's the one with all the
true blue friends?
    The confidant—Magi

Just who exactly, are all
those people?
    They're me—Margaret Michel-ley!

—Michelle Owen

Scenes from Seat 32F

Whose voice smiles as he announces
the temperature?
        Capt. Richards
Whose cough sounds harsh, even above
roaring engines?
         The illegal
         smoker up
         front with ash
         colored hair.

Whose constant calls attract down
casting glances?
         Some irritable
         red head in
         seat 31.

Who fusses with the tray, the light, and
the chair?
         That bear-
         clutching child.

Who is afraid of landing and has ears
that are popping?
         Hmmm . . .

                —Lori Morency

Attention

Do you love me, Mom?
  Mmhmm.
Did you have a good day, Mom?
  Mmhmm.
What's for dinner, Mom?
  Mmhmm.
Do you see that big fuchsia green alien
  sitting in your lap, Mom?
  Mmhmm.
So, can I go out tonight, Mom?
      NO

               —Allison Boye

Generations

Who was strong and silent and carried a gun in his coat
    pocket on midnight calls?
      Father

Who closed like a flower at sunset and never let anyone
    know her?
      Mother

Who ruled from his bed, his gray sickness seeping through the
    cracks, silencing the house?
      Grandfather

Who pouted in her room, injured, when she was the one who
    broke hearts with words?
      Grandmother

Who wandered the bean rows at dawn in her nightgown wet with
    dew, wearing a beret and pretending not to be perfect?
      Little girl

Who stalks my nights from room to room, never letting go?
      Ghosts

—Gerry Jones

Self-Pity

Why do I feel like crying?
    Vacation is over
    Carol's father listed as critical
    The needy cousin inherited nothing
    The old dog has fleas
    My husband never asks to read my poems
    It's raining
    New York takes five hours to cross
    School starts in ten days
    A grown man won't wear his seat belt
    I stood at Alcott's grave yesterday

—Luana Russell

Samantha is a high school student
at Murphy High in Santa Barbara, CA.
She is taking a math test
hoping to pass to become a senior
as if it was her life
at one-thirty in the afternoon

—Yasmeen Shorish

Whispers that fall
on that summer's night
across the meadow
Someone is lying cold
the broken bushes, the bright light
Cristine is going home.

—Jessica Adkins

Am I teaching because I never grew up, because I can't do, or
    because I am not 6'8" tall?
Should I do what I think is right or compromise to those who want
    analysis, tightening, more grades in my grade book?
How long should I watch my friend follow the wrong path to sure
    disappointment, destruction, and isolation?
Am I batting first, third, or eighth, or am I on the bench, a defensive
    replacement?
What league am I in?
Am I moving or is everything moving around me?
Where are the boundaries?
How far should I pursue the ideal?

—Bob Coleman

Blues

Who says blue's for
melancholy?
Not me.
Not here.

I crunch through marsh grass
    side-stepping a sea of
    blue-twinkling
    new-blooming marsh heather.

I stoop for a tide-tossed mussel shell,
    trace my finger along
    blue-grey swirls inside a
    pearlsmooth rim.

I spy faroff hydrangea
    balls bouncing
    blue above
    old stone boulders.

I pluck the sweetness of
    blueberries from
    blue-heavy branches,
    blue-splashed bushes.

I eavesdrop on
    bluejays scolding
    a cloud-patched sky
    a wave-rumpled river.

Don't sing those blues
    for me
    not in August
    not in my blue world.

             —Sheila G. Murphy

Interlude

Don Quixote and Sancho Panza

Once you get questions and answers going, you begin to nudge yourself toward creating characters, maybe one wise and one simple—or maybe the wise one really is the simple one—it all depends.

Even brief questions can become profound, and a whole reverberation of talk can follow. It feels easy to ask the questions, and then, in answering, some enticing angles begin to appear. What one person says identifies that person, reflects on the content and quality of the mind behind the talk. There is no way for the character to hide—the reader will begin to assess the speaker.

No need to protect anyone—let the developing characters speak for themselves, and that means letting them be distinctive, have insights and oddities, be full of surprises. No quirk is too ridiculous or surprising, no insight too profound.

Your puppets can ask, answer, converse, discover, redeem, take off on their own into the poetry forms we are practicing.

Syllable Count Poems

Introduction

The "play" or "tension" between *form* and *language* is at the heart of syllable-count poems. A formal poem such as a sonnet says, "Here are my rules; deal with me." And language tries to behave wonderfully in spite of the sonnet's usual "rules": fourteen lines, iambic pentameter, and you can add others.

Gimme a break! you say. Isn't writing fine words and making sharp images tough enough? We have to battle form as well?

No. *You do it because you want to.* Remember the pantoum? Wasn't it fun, in a painful sort of way? You take on the challenge of a formal poem, trying to overcome its rules without looking like a klutz.

An example: A key aspect of form is the length of the line. There are different ways of measuring line-length. Look hard at the beginning lines of this sonnet written in the mid-1600s by John Milton:

> Avenge O Lord Thy slaughtered Saints, whose bones (1)
> Lie scatter'd on the Alpine mountains cold . . .   (2)

We think of four ways of measuring those lines:

(1) Line 1 *looks* longer than line 2. (Yup. Sure does.)

(2) Line 1 has more words—eight—than line 2's *seven*. (Agreed.)

(3) Both lines have *ten* syllables. Count them out:
  a$_{(1)}$venge$_{(2)}$ O$_{(3)}$ Lord$_{(4)}$ . . .

(4) Both lines have (or can be made to have) *five* accents or "beats":
  lie SCAT-ter'd ON the AL-pine MOUN-tains COLD

Poets are interested in all four ways of measuring, but most *formal poets* measure by beats. For example, they follow the five beat/line rule of the sonnet. But whether or not they're writing poems with preset rules (like the sonnet and pantoum), most poets also care about how poems look on the page, how they read to the eye, and (most important) how they sound.

A poem's "measurements" affect such things. Physical shape is part of a poem's meanings. Getting good words into a perfectly measured line is satisfying. It feels good when a line looks, reads, and sounds right.

But form is a tough foe. Unrelenting. We know you remember haiku from third grade. So show us a *wonderful* one, we say. Formal poems will take your best shots. And formal measurements create problems, too.

Rhyme is an aspect of form, and it creates terrible problems in many beginners' poems. Not that beginners *can't* rhyme. It's that they can! Beginners will find and use rhyming words, whether they fit or not. You've seen poems where "wrong" words have been used simply because they rhyme. So we say, *hold off rhyme, for a time.* (Sorry.)

Dealing with *measurement* is less simple. Trying to follow a certain number of counts can lead to padded, "fat" lines—to lines with excess baggage. Say the form we are following calls for 8-syllable lines, but what we need to say can be said in six syllables:

> It seems a whirly sport.   (6 syllables)

We toss in a couple of syllables more, to "fatten" the line out to eight:

> It seems *to be* a whirly sport.   (8 syllables)

Also, a line's pre-set length can lead the poet to cut so many syllables and words that what's left is incomprehensible: Here's such a line, for us:

> Changed blood the garden stops.   (Wha'?)

Ending lines at the point required by a formal pattern creates other problems. There are no hard and fast rules on how lines should end. (Show us a rule, we'll show you a poet who violates it. Successfully.) Still, one of us favors line breaks that

> end with important words or syllables;
> stimulate interest in what's coming next;
> end in ways that are *not* usual or expected;
> "sound good" aloud—often nouns and verbs, least often
> words like *with, and, to, from, would, shall, as, is,* _____

Here, for practice in measuring and counting, you'll work with **syllables.** Easier to count than accents, harder to count than words, syllable counting is perfect!

Work to do: We want you to draft a haiku, a cinquain, and a "number poem." In addition, for anyone needing/wanting "extra credit," we offer the opportunity to write a "Higgledy-Piggledy."

(A what? That sure sounds silly.)

Haiku Steps

A haiku usually *follows the form of seventeen syllables* arranged in three lines. Forgive us this example:

Step 1.

Bad Haiku?

A haiku usually	(5 syllables)
follows the form of seven-	(7)
teen syllables a-	(5)

How 'bout that? Did we just dash off a haiku? Well maybe. Of a sort. But read it aloud. Neither beautiful nor sensible, "Bad Haiku?" does seem to follow one aspect of form—the syllable count. Can you "hear" five syllables in line one? But see? Even counting syllables isn't automatic.

Here, needing a five-syllable first line, we forced *usually* into two-syllables (**yews**-zhlee). If we'd needed a seven-syllable line, we might have pretended *usually* was four syllables long: **yew**-zhu-uh-lee. Most speakers make two [**yews**-zhlee] or three [**yews**-zhu-lee] syllables of the word. But in any case, the number of syllables in a word isn't always simple.

How many syllables do **yew** make when you pronounce "mystery" aloud? The point: Don't fret. As you work, pronounce your written words in your usual way and try to catch the number of syllables.

What we did in writing "Bad Haiku?" was to take words from a sentence and lay them out in syllables—5, 7, 5. There's more to haiku than that. Here's a more serious try:

Text 33

Line	Syllables	**Spring**
1	X X X X X	White crocuses rise
2	X X X X X X X	porcelain handles from earth—
3	X X X X X	spouting butterflies

We observed the line and syllable pattern, and also tried to find good images—the idea of a <u>crocus</u> as a <u>water faucet handle.</u> And (as do most traditional haiku) ours hints at a season of the year: "White crocuses rise."

Step 2.

For your haiku draft . . .

Look around you, senses alert, for an image that has something a little special about it: it reminds you of something; it has possibilities; it somehow touches you. Don't ignore hearing, smelling, tasting.

As you begin to get words, find related words/images that suggest a season: "*Snow*" suggests winter—but perhaps too obviously. *An orange moon* or *sounds of a football game* might more subtly suggest fall; *a cicada's trill* or *the smell of burning charcoal,* summer; *a firefly* or *a kite,* spring. A change (e.g., color or condition or movement) in some natural thing (tree, sky, grass, bodies of water) can suggest a season.

As you play against the haiku form, cut unnecessary words. SUCH AS? Look back at Text 33. Did we goof, leaving in the adjective "white"? Isn't there already a sense of "white" in "porcelain"? When possible cut out such words as *and*, *but*, *a* or *an*, and *the*.

Another way to describe haiku comes from poet Robert King. Most haiku, he says, have a two-part structure: a specific image and an "over-arching" general statement. For example, this poem by Basho:

Text 34

On a withered branch   [specific image]
A crow has settled—
Autumn nightfall   [more general statement]
        —Basho

In this translation, Basho's poem breaks the 17-syllable pattern. Patterns are made to be broken. *But at the start, stick to the pattern awhile.*

Cinquain Steps

Step 1.

Early in the twentieth century, perhaps in response to Japanese syllabic forms, Adelaide Crapsey invented the cinquain (pronounced sing-CANE). Like the haiku, the cinquain often features a single strong image from nature. One obvious way to find that image is by close observation of the natural world, letting yourself make connections with other images, feelings, and activities: e.g., rain puddling on a sidewalk producing thoughts of unkept promises; a gray sky suggesting the angry faces of ancestors.

Step 2.

The sequence is simple—lines of two, four, six, eight, and two syllables. Five lines altogether. There tends to be a rhythmical pattern, too, the da-DAH da-DAH rhythm called "iambic." If making such a rhythm seems a worthy challenge, go for it. More important, try to move toward a lift or surprise at the end.

Here's a draft of our cinquain: # of syllables

Beneath	(2)
a picnic bench	(4)
small red ants dance waltzes	(6)
in praise of harvest gods who sent	(8)
the feast.	(2)

From ants at a picnic, our thoughts moved to peoples (e.g., plains Indians) whose gods were celebrated and prayed to. We counted the syllables right, got a noticeable iambic rhythm in lines 1 and 2 (be-NEATH / a PIC-nic BENCH) and in 4 and 5. All of which makes line 3—what? Here's how it sounds read in iambs: small RED ants DANCE waltz-ES

Hmmm. Not only is the rhythm off, the words are too. "Small" is fat—an unnecessary word. Who ever hear of *giant* red ants?

"Dance waltzes" is also fat: *waltz* (one syllable) does the work of *dance waltzes* (three syllables). Line 3 is a mess, and even line 4 is less than perfect. Start again?

No. We were once privileged to watch a corn dance in New Mexico. Are there fruitful connections between ants, "dancing" for what their picnicking "gods" leave behind, and the rich harvest ceremonial of pueblo Indians? Back to work on line 3.

	The IN-sects DANCE their DANCE
(or)	The RED ants DANCE their WALTZ
(or)	The ANTS dance TAR-an-TEL-as

Tarantella. tar-an-TEL-la. What does the word mean? It's a dance of some kind. A good-sounding word, too—although it makes the line count out to 7-syllables. Still, we look in our dictionary: "a vigorous folk dance; couples dancing with tambourines." Not exactly what we hoped for. "A dancing mania." Hmmm, we think. Closer. We imagine the frenzied picnicking of ants. "It was believed that the dancing mania was caused by bites of tarantula spiders." (At the very least, we're interested.)

Text 35

Thanks

Beneath
our picnic bench
a tarantella dance
by ants, to careless gods who sent
their feast.

Not perfect, perhaps, but hey! Thanks, form. Text 35 needed your lift.

"Number Poem" Steps

Step 1.

Base your number poem on a sequence of numbers important to you —a Social Security number, a zip code, a date (written in numerals: e.g., 10-31-1924), an address, telephone number, lucky numbers. . . . The sequence you choose sets the pattern of syllables for your poem.

Here's an example, based on a telephone number: 636-4075. (For the 0, we'll use 10.)

Text 36

(Line #)	(Syllables)	Call
(1)	X XXX X X	Tacked alongside this phone
(2)	X X X	a friend's face.
(3)	X XX X X	I cannot say his name
(4)	X X X X	yet know him well.
(5)	X X X XX X X X	One night he disappeared, as light from fire,
(6)	X X X X X X X	went out for good. Still, I'll
(7)	X X X X X	know him when he calls.

Step 2.   To get language for your poem, *jot down images and scenes that connect with your number:* people, faces, actions, moments, scenes. Then, lay out your pattern of lines and syllables, as above. Work "the meat" of your jottings into your pattern, changing language as necessary to fit the counts. In short, *connect content and form.*

Step 3.   **In your Notebook:** From your three syllable-count drafts—the haiku, the cinquain, and the number poem—choose your favorite. *Reading aloud often as you work, edit the poem, making a new copy, and copy it into your notebook.* If there's something a reader should know about the poem (e.g., where the numbers for your number poem came from), tell that too.

Now for Those Wanting "Extra Credit"

Enjoy syllable counts? Have we got a deal for you! The "Higgledy-Piggledy" is a fun kind of poem based on syllables arranged into what are called "dactyls." HIG-gle-dy (/uu) is a dactyl; HIG-gle-dy PIG-gle-dy is a *double*-dactyl. And "Double-dactyl" is this poem's formal name.

You can have fun making your first line of nonsense "fit" the rest of the poem. Other lines may make you wish you'd never heard of "double-dactyls." Altogether only eight lines long, six of the eight lines in the "Higgledy-Piggledy" are double-dactyls.

Higgledy-Piggledy Steps

Some lines of the Higgledy-Piggledy come easily. The first line, for example: you can use any nonsense you want—as long as your "words" set the rhythm. (Say them aloud; you'll hear it.)

Step 1.   HIG-gle-dy PIG-gle-dy   (/uu /uu)
              BIP-a-dee BOP-a-dee
Step 2.   TICK-a-loo TACK-a-loo

The hardest/most important thing to "find" is a name that will become the focus of your Higgledy-Piggledy. THIS NAME MUST BE A DOUBLE-DACTYL (of sorts). Ideally, the name you find will both be famous and a double-dactyl. There are great composers (Ludwig van Beethoven—LUD-wig van BEET-hov-en), presidents (Benjamin Harrison), presidents' wives (Eleanor Roosevelt), and congressmen (Senator Magnuson). There are old poets galore: Emily Dickinson, Muriel Rukeyser, Ralph Waldo Emerson, and Alfred, Lord Tennyson.

If you take slight liberties with famous names, the list grows fast: Margaret Thatcher-o (for Margaret Thatcher), Henery Kissinger (for Henry Kissinger), John FitzG Kennedy (for JFK). An easy trick for preserving at least a semblance of the double-dactyl rhythm is to add a middle initial to some famous name—whether the person has one or not. Susan B. Anthony does. But Ernest Q. Hemingway? You'll think of artists and athletes, musicians and movie stars with double-dactyl names.

Do you hear the double-dactyl rhythms? *Read them aloud until you do.*

A *guaranteed* source for double-dactyl names is friends and acquaintances. Good old Gwendolyn and Cassius, Jennifer and Anthony, Marilyn and Samuel. If their last names don't already fit, make them. But do so in good humor. (Know us? William E. Stafford-y and A. Stephen Dunning-er. Now don't say anything mean.)

Step 3. Once you have a name to work with, *brainstorm a few facts and ideas that connect with it.* Why, you may even have to look something up. Then study the Higgledy-Piggledy form. (We've underline places where form produces an unnatural reading.)

Text 37 DENISON VENISON

(1)	Denison, Venison	Nonsense dactyls **/uu /uu**
(2)	Alfred, Lord Tennyson	Famous person's name
(3)	<u>wrote</u> fancy poems such as	(Ordinarily: wrote FAN-cy)
(4)	"Tears, idle tears"	Short line: **/uu/**
(5)	<u>Which</u> hasn't much to do	(Ordinarily: Which HAS-n't)
(6)	coincidentally	One-word double-dactyl
(7)	with the task facing you:	
(8)	You must shift gears!	Rhyming short line.

Details of Higgledy-Piggledy Forms

Poem is two quatrains (two 4-line stanzas) long.
There's a stanza break between lines 4 and 5.
Lines 1, 2, 3, and 5, 6, and 7 are double-dactyls (**/uu /uu**)
Lines 4 and 8 have a four-syllable **/uu/** rhythm.
Also, the end words of lines 4 and 8 rhyme (*tears* and *gears*).
In stanza 1, line 2 consists of your double-dactyl.
In stanza 2, either line 6 or line 7 is a one-word double-dactyl.

Read aloud (and maybe use?) these nice, one-word double-dactyls:

characteristically (CHAR-ac-ter-IS-tic-ly [/uu/uu])
ultra-conservative (UL-tra-con-SERV-a-tive [/uu/uu])

valedictorian	polysyllabic'ly
organizational	uncomplimentary
heterosexual	idiosyncrasy
Mediterranean	impractability
over-emphatic'ly	counter-intelligence
undiplomatic'ly	irritability
anachronistic'ly	verisimilitude

(Yeah, they're a mouthful.) *But what if . . .* What if you have trouble finding that one-word double-dactyl for line 6 or 7? Well, just as we fudged a little on names for line 2, we can fudge a little on the one-word double-dactyl. In our first draft of Text 37, we somewhat desperately used "not-unexpectedly" as a one-word double-dactyl. Poetic license?

Step 4.   *Finish the poem.* Don't let it grow too serious: its rhythm is too playful for that. When finished with a draft, consider revising your first-line nonsense words to fit your poem (even more) perfectly.

We said Higgledy-Piggledy would be fun. We *didn't* say it would be easy.

You follow the "outside" rules of a poetry form because you want to. It's fun. A challenge. Again, think back to the pantoum. Rules for its repeating lines (like the rules for the patterns of several kinds of sonnets) evolved over time. It's all right *not* to write sonnets, pantoums, or even Higgledy-Piggledy's, but . . . if you're going to write one, and have others agree that what you've written is this form or that, you should probably follow its rules. More or less.

Poems in Response

775-9184

The phone sits here, black and hard
as charcoal waiting to flame
when you call me up
and your words begin their hot, bright fires.
Well,
nothing's burning now at this end.
Afraid? Afraid?

—Robert King

NIGHT SOUNDS

And now
The cricket chirps
Outside my door again—
His song will pierce my thoughts and dreams
Tonight.

—Glynn Bridgewater

Please Remember

If the phone rings
after midnight,
with a lonesome
voice calling to
you, please remember there is
someone far from home tonight who
needs your words of friendship.

—Sadie Tirmizi
(444–4786)

Phone

If you
would
like to know my phone number, you

will need to
count the syllables in each sentence.
With what you get there

you could
call
me up.
It might be no one's home.

                              —Amanda LaFond

To See

I must see
beauty in the lava
waves, the slate grey
sky, the chocolate mousse

foaming at the shoreline,
mussels stretching
black tongues on plastic milk
cartons, like

claws waving
goodbye; where are the star
fish of my youth?
the blue waves, infinite

shells thrashing at my feet
beaten by egg
whites, beating the shoreline
I must see

                              Jersey Shore, 1991

                              —Nancy Gorrell
                                 (b. 3-6-46)

Wait, Wish, & Wonder

I sit and wait
and wonder
when he'll smile at me again.
Alone,
I wish his lips would say
my name, over and over
like a dream.

                              —Dori Steavens

Strength, power, and might,
Soaring on wings of the wind,
The mighty eagle.

—Carey Rollins

Collegiate Autumn

Prof. H. clears his throat
amid leather smells. Outside,
trees' last days of green.

—Emilynn J. Pumarega

Drilliamson, Quilliamson

Drilliamson, Quilliamson
Winifred Williamson
dug through some bushes
and buried her snout.

Angering the Labrador
quite-unexpectedly,
porcupine pointers were
all that came out.

—Kimberly Williamson

The 1991 International Special Olympics Opening Ceremonies
or
Homeboy

Danderson, Manderson
Richard Dean Anderson
walked through the Dome with a
bright, charming smile.

Special Olympians
characteristically
reached out to welcome him—
home for a while.

—Cris Anderson

Tillingworth, Millingworth

Tillingworth, Millingworth,
Old Roger Chillingworth
Made Arthur miserable
Day after day.

Hester and Pearl survived
So independently,
Mother-and-daughter-ly
Flaunting that <u>A.</u>

—Sheila G. Murphy

POPEYE

Jailerman, nailerman
Popeye the Sailorman:
smooched Sweet Pea, punched Bluto,
saved Olive Oyl.

"Strong to the finish 'cause
melodramatically,
I eats me spinach for
Olive, me goil!"

—Laura Treacy Bentley

Interlude

The Revolt of the Syllables

We never met a syllable we didn't like. Each one, you know, has a meaning; that is, its associations in words we use one place will hover over into another place. There is no way to escape the effects of sound, syllable, sequence. You might as well make friends with these lurking sounds.

And one way is to force yourself to look both ways between words, make a pattern that requires you to be alert for options that aren't the first options but are something further that you must seek out in order to satisfy a rule you have adopted.

"Then what happens to content?" "Won't my meaning get distorted?" "Will I be, in fact, dishonest?" That could be, but you are practicing; you are exploring. And you are finding out that language is ready to help or hurt. People who are unaware lie even when they are trying to tell the truth, for their language clutters up their intention: their readers or hearers can't close in on a clear communication.

The pressure you are learning to put on your language will make it convey something nearer to your true being. That is the faith of a person who uses craft, of a <u>good</u> person who uses craft. And that is the way you should be.

Dream-Write 3

Introduction

We've called our own dream-writes garbage ("gar-BAHZ").

But why should we ask *you* to waste time practicing "bad writing"?

The answer lies in what that practice can offer. *Sometimes dream-writes can lead you to words and images that are important, words and images you cannot "get to" by conscious mental activity. By thinking.*

Remember, we said *sometimes.*

Much of the writing we do in life is thoughtful and planned. Even if we're only thinking, "Have to write two pages for history class," we know the general subject is "Segregation": We're writing about *something*. Other times we plan with outline, notes, the whole schmear. Even lists (e.g., "Things to do," "People to ask") have "subjects" built in, before we start making them. Letters have reasons for being written, too: things to tell, things to ask.

For most of our writing we can think and plan and outline and (on our best days) write something that's logical and clear. Get the job done.

Dream-write goes the opposite direction. It doesn't have any subject—except what comes. It's spontaneous and unplanned. It doesn't set out to make sense. And it's more psychological (subconscious) than logical (conscious).

It has no job to do.

SO WHY DREAM-WRITE?

Because dream-writes may give us glimpses deep into ourselves. We get another slant on who and what we are, different from all the "normal" reflections we get from our families, our friends, from school, from "the media." *Once in a while,* dream-writes take us inside our brains and hearts, where some of our best writing comes from.

THAT'S WHY. By imitating dreams, we get access to parts of our selves that we can't get through logic, through planning, or through thinking.

(OK, that's a pretty good reason.)

But you'll notice we've been careful not to guarantee too much for dream-writes. We've used words like "sometimes" and phrases like "Once in a while" in describing how "unreliable" dream-writes are. And we call our own dream-writes "gar-BAHZ."

There are no guarantees, but there is this belief: Going through the dream-write steps may lead to that thing-like-poem you value above all others. That's what other writers tell us. That's what can happen.

Dream-Write Steps

Step 1.

Find your dream-writes (ten or more) and *divide them into "approximately equal" piles*—the "good ones," the others. ("Good" describes those that surprise and interest you most.) If the piles are uneven, that's OK.

Read the "good" pile. Then find a pen or pencil, place it in your writing hand, and re-read these dream-writes, *finding at least three "little chunks" that interest you. Little chunks* could mean something so small as a word or two, and probably nothing larger than five to eight words.

These chunks can be "about" anything. They need not make sense.

Simply, they interest you.

Step 2.

Copy this handful of chunks onto a fresh page.

Now, instead of writing fast, WRITE SLOWLY. Make *at least* two pages of "slow-write" from your little chunks. How?

Answer these questions. (Put one of your chunks in blanks 1, 2, and 3. Use the same or different chunks for the blanks. Whatever seems best.)

(a) What else can I say about [1] _____?

(b) What does [2] _____ remind me of?

(c) What would _____ (name of some person, living or dead, real or imagined) say about [3] _____?

Some writers actually copy question (a), (b), or (c) into their slow-write—a reminder to themselves of what they're focusing on.

Step 3.

Again, with pencil/pen in hand, read aloud what you've written. (If there's someone you can work with on this, all the better.) As you read, *underline or circle parts* that make you "see" and other parts that hit your ear as important.

We're expecting you to find in your slow-write images, words, and phrases that might be the bones of a poem.

Step 4.

Then *copy onto a fresh place those marked parts.* How do they read? Anything there to connect? <u>Anything</u> there?

Dream-Write 4

Introduction

You have practiced writing fast, have selected "nuggets" from your most dream-like writing, and (using the "expansion questions") have practiced writing out (slow-writing) from those nuggets. Then you cut them to the bone.

You've done a bunch!

So what's the result at this point? *Perhaps* a few lines that interest you. A few bones for a thing-like-poem. *Perhaps* a mishmash that interests you hardly at all. Most likely, something in between.

How to continue with dream-write?

Dream-Write Steps

Step 1.

If you're interested in the raw material that dream-write has produced so far, continue working with it.

HERE'S ONE WAY:

(a) From Dream-Write 3, Step 4, you have a few essential words, images, and phrases. *Nuggets. Bones.* (OK, little "winners" from the gar-BAHZ.) *Right?* You fast-wrote, then selected a few nuggets.

(b) Starting from those nuggets, slow-write from the Q's we suggested—for example, "What else can I say about _____?"

(c) Still the process isn't over. If your slow-write interests you even a little, remove a few of its basic bones and lay them out "poem-like" on a fresh page.

(d) Then expand on that skeleton. And once they're expanded, . . .

YES! You're into the process. Expanding, then cutting down, expanding, cutting down. *It's as if you were playing an accordion —stretching, squeezing, stretching, squeezing. It may take more than one stretch and squeeze to get the full, rich tune. That is, the poem.*

As you work, expanding and contracting, new associations (only some of them fitting) will try to enter your work. Old stuff will drop out because it doesn't seem important enough or "musical" enough or fitting.

Got it? Fast-write to nuggets to slow-write to nuggets, expand and contract . . . *Why a person could spend a lifetime on this process!*

Here's a review of questions for use in slow-writing from the nuggets. As you work, adjust them so they fit:

(a) What else can I say about [1] _____?

(b) What does [2] _____ remind me of?

(c) What would [3] _____(name of some person, living or dead, real or imagined) say about [4] _____?

Write fully from these questions, taking your time. Use all three questions, if you can. If you find yourself getting away from true feelings, ask:

(d) *How do I really feel about* _____?

Finally, here's an example of our getting the process underway:

NUGGETS FROM OUR DREAM-WRITE:
Aunt Dudu's Ford
tearing Whitney's shirt (and so forth)

SLOW-WRITING FROM OUR NUGGETS. (USING THE Q'S)
(What else can I say about that Ford?)
I was the first nephew to ride in the new Ford. A black coupé. Junior tried to edge me out, but Aunt Dudu was big on playing "fair" and I was touching the car door before Junior got there. It was cloudy, and Dudu worried about getting the Ford rained on. We drove toward Pike Lake and Dudu started turning around. I said something hopeful like, "We could go to Pike Lake," and Dudu said, "I'll bet Junior's boiling by now." That same week, our spaniel Glen died . . .

CUTTING TO THE SKELETON
I was first in the Ford that cloudy day heading for Pike Lake Road. Back home Junior burned. Then Glen died . . .

Writing-out and cutting may take you far away from those nuggets of yours. *That's OK!* They're still there—perhaps buried again under new rememberings and imaginings, perhaps covered up by your sense of what's public and what's private.

Step 2.   If you're uninterested in the nuggets you mined from dream-writes, start fresh. Start with scratch paper, a little time, and try again to fast-write your way into mistakes, revelations, and other surprises.
But if it hasn't worked so far! you say,

HOW MUCH TIME SHOULD I WASTE?

We don't mean to blow your mind, but . . .
We think you should try it many more times. Eight or ten or more! Yes, the entire process—(a) collecting dream-writes, (b) mining the nuggets, (c) writing-out slowly, using the questions, and (d) cutting to the bone.

We're talking about lots of work. And since we're trying to help here, not to interfere, let us say again *why* repeating the entire process many times might be worth the effort.

Getting poems from dream-writes is admittedly inefficient. It takes lots of writing, expanding, and cutting to get the dream-write poem. All that gar-BAHZ! But again, the poem that gets its start—or a key image—from dream-write might be the very poem you value most.

And that's because through dreams (and through dream-write) **you sometimes get material you can't get any other way.**

Waking UP

Some writers worry that the "nuggets" from the dream-write process are unconnected. "They don't fit together." It will sometimes seem that way.

An opposite view holds that bits of dreams (like nuggets from dream-writes) do have a kind of fit—*if only the dreamer (the writer) is open to it.*

Smack dab in the middle of your images from a hike in the woods appears an image of spilling french fries at a fast-food restaurant. So far as is possible, trust the image. And let the connection come, if it will. The reason it might come is that in dreams, as in dream-write, the maker of the images (you) is a consistent, whole person.

French fries and forest trees connect because you connect.

It takes practice to write swiftly enough that you approximate dreams. You have strong instincts against accepting whatever comes up in the writing, against writing carelessly, against revealing too much.

Still, the stuff of dreams is friendly to poems. Good poems move as dreams move, without all the usual connections. Like dreams, good poems present fresh images and connect old images in new ways.

And good poems work toward truth, as do dreams.

Interlude

Using Tricks to Find Out Who You Are

One of the most remarkable writers who ever lived, Sören Kierkegaard, had the idea that if he wrote fast enough he could keep from being false. He wouldn't have time to put in those hesitations and evasions that his calculating self used to interrupt the clear, honest impulse of an innocent inner being.

You know what we mean? If you are calculating on the effect you want to create, where are your own primary impulses in life? You will start by hoodwinking others and end by not having a true self of your own. Somehow, you have to keep the real you alive. It's a challenge, especially these days. Kierkegaard glimpsed that, and his writing came to be a lifelong, serious attempt to achieve subjective integrity.

Dream-writes make a move in the direction of such a serious objective, even as they ask for little bits of language accepted uncritically. We must preserve that openness, no matter how adept we become in our writing.

Memory Map 2

Introduction

In Memory Map 1 you went back to an earlier time in your life, focusing on your sleeping place. **Memory Map 2** focuses on your neighborhood. Neighborhood? Some say a neighborhood is a physical place with *general* boundaries. "My 'hood's west of town." Others agree that it's a place, but (like what's called "turf") one with *definite* boundaries. Others say that neighborhood is an attitude or "frame of mind," where people tend to be accepting and protective of one another.

Some say you have to live in a place a while before you think of it as your neighborhood. Others say a neighborhood simply is—with its **features**—this well-known building, that intersection, the joining of two rivers—and its **customs**—sitting on the front steps summer evenings, keeping dogs on leashes, being suspicious of strangers: the 'hood is there for the newcomer who wants it and seems to fit in.

The nearest neighbors of a farm family in Colorado or South Dakota might live miles away. What is **their** neighborhood? Urban neighbors might live above you, below you, down the hall, or just the other side of a four-inch wall. Someone living in a foreign city has a very different neighborhood from someone living in Los Angeles or Omaha. Someone's neighborhood in rural Alabama is very different from that of someone living on a reservation in Wyoming. It's probably true that some people's neighborhoods are "measured in inches," others in miles. *Something* binds a neighborhood together—shared religious or ethnic backgrounds, economic and social situations, common recreations, *et cetera.*

Go ahead, think a while about your neighborhood—"where" it is, its **boundaries,** what binds it together, its features and customs. Think about your own role in your neighborhood: whether you're at its center or its outside edge? Discuss neighborhoods with others. How you define your 'hood and how you feel toward it will affect how your poem turns out. But it's also true that no one definition of neighborhood is required for a good poem, nor is any one set of feelings.

Text 38

The 1st

What I remember about that day
is boxes stacked across the walk
and couch springs curling through the air
and drawers and tables balanced on the curb

and us, hollering,
leaping up and around
happy to have a playground;
nothing about the emptied rooms
nothing about the emptied family
—Lucille Clifton

Read the poem aloud, if you haven't already. What does the title, "The 1st," suggest? What feelings about neighborhood do you get from the poem? What's your response to the repetitions in the last two lines?

(Bear with us. We know what follows is old stuff for you. But we want you to **take your time** with this getting-ready-to-write step. As you work, **try closing your eyes each time we ask you to "see."**)

Think back again to where you lived when you were four or five or six. (Of course, you may still live there.) If you can't remember so far back, or don't want to, go to another age, say eight or ten. "See" your 'hood, the building you lived in. (Does closing your eyes help?) Try to get the size, shape and color of that building. Even if you still live there, imagine yourself inside the room where you slept. Notice/ Remember where things are—furniture, doors, and windows. "See" yourself in that room. See yourself in your clothes from back then. Watch "that younger you" move around that room. What are you doing? See yourself doing things you did back then. Catch the expression on your face.

Now look out the window from that sleeping place. What's the view? Do you see part of your old neighborhood? Are you looking out on the front? The back? One side? Where does the sun rise? Where does it set? Look up, look down, look all around: Who/ What do you see? Such natural things as sky, trees, and grass? Buildings, fences, cars?

Looking out that "back then" window, you probably saw part of what you consider your neighborhood. Was what you "saw" a major or minor part of your 'hood? If possible, find someone whose "neighborhood-back-then" was very different from your own. Talk more about neighborhoods.

Especially, listen carefully as others tell about theirs. Try to decide what makes a neighborhood. Decide how far your neighborhood stretches, and how you fit into it.

Consider: Are neighbors necessarily "neighborly"?

Memory Map Steps

On a fresh sheet of paper, *draw a map of your neighborhood* when you were four or five or six. Use the "bird's eye view," as if you are looking down from above. Label things that might not otherwise be

Step 1. clear. Include important "natural things": bushes, water, an important tree. If you forget some person's name, or where something goes, cut yourself some slack: MAKING UP (IMAGINING) IS OK.

If you still live where you lived then, "correct for changes" over the years. Again, if going back to the age of four to six isn't comfortable, choose another time; but neighborhoods *earlier* than four to six seem to work less well than *later* neighborhoods. Or if you feel like it, INVENT A NEIGHBORHOOD.

Put in the basic stuff—streets, buildings, key places. Check out our map, on the next page.

Step 2. With the basics in place, add twelve or more "personal specifics" to your neighborhood map. Here's how.

First, check out our **"Item List"** below. Select any items that connect with your neighborhood and tell about it. Twenty+ WORDS. PAST TENSE.

Item List Where did the sun rise?
Were there pets in your neighborhood?
What was it like out in front of your place? Out in back?
Where did you play alone? What did you play?
Where did you play with others? What?
Was there music in your neighborhood? What kind? Who played it?
Where did that nice person live? Who was it? The exact address?
What was that smell? Where did it come from?
Tell about the haunted (spooky, scary, mysterious) building/house.
What interesting (wild, sad) thing happened one holiday?
Who was the bully? What did (s)he do to bully people?
Where's the place you liked best? Tell why.
What special things did you eat? Where did you get it? Was it good?
Where did you go when you ran away, or pretended to?
Where were the dangerous places?
What could you hear when you stood in this one place?
Where did you see animals? Tell about them.
Where could you collect things? What things?
Tell about the place you were afraid to go to.
Tell about the person you felt sorry for.

Here's how we answered the first question: *"Where did the sun rise?"*

> The sun rose over the pines in Molly Atwater's big yard. I had to squint into it those mornings Molly and I played catch. (24 words.)

The second: *"Were there pets in your neighborhood?"*

> Magraws tied their mean dog Princess here, but they used a long rope and she could almost get us when we went by. (23 words.)

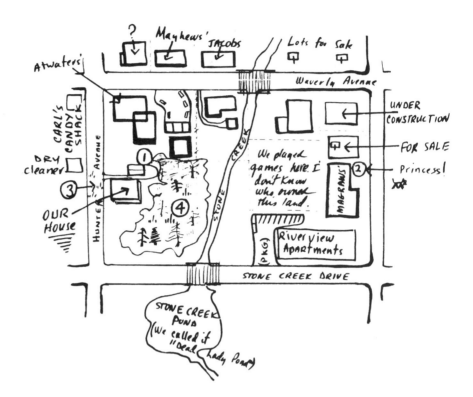

① The sun rose over the pines in Molly Atwater's big yard....

② Magraws tied their mean dog Princess here, but they...

③ The sidewalk was full of cracks with weeds coming through, and bumpy...

④ Birch and pine trees! Sherwood forest and an African jungle, and... (I don't draw the world's best tree. ☺)

Map 2

The third: *"What was it like out front of your place?"*

> The sidewalk was full of cracks with weeds coming through, and bumpy places. Only Lee Magraw was good enough to skip rope there. (23 words)

Each time you finish an answer, number it and also put its number *where it belongs* on your map. (See the circled numbers 1, 2, 3 on our map.)

Once you've taken what you can use from our Item List, add other stuff of your own. Tell about people, experiences, events **not** suggested by our Item List. Continue writing twenty+ words for each. Number each completed item and enter its number on your map.

Altogether, *write up a total of twelve or more items.*

Step 3. The goal for this exercise is a three- (or four-, or more) stanza poem based on your map and your written material.

If you're eager to get going without further advice, start now: (a) Focus your poem on important events from your map. (b) Try using a repeating line (or refrain) to begin or end each chunk. (c) Cut your twenty+ word items to the bone.

If you're patient (and this is how we hope you'll feel), let us help you accomplish three similar goals: (a) finding a thematic pattern for your poem, or imposing one, (b) writing a line from that pattern to be used as "a refrain," and (c) cutting words from your written-out items.

Depending on the complexity of your numbered items and on how you view them, your neighborhood poem may focus on one or on many events. (That is, you might base an entire poem on someone's [something's] disappearance, or on an important confrontation or event. On the other hand, you might use a group of events that create a pattern somehow—different neighborhood recreations, for example.)

Look over your map and your written-out items. Is one of those items so strong that you want to focus your poem on it? *If so, you may need to jot down more images and details connecting with it.*

Or can you, among your dozen-or-more items, *find some kind of pattern?* That three or four items are about neighborhood *people,* for example, or about *a certain individual or family.* Or about certain ACTIVITIES—games, meeting places, traditions. Perhaps some are based on FEELINGS, such as good times, bad times, sweet times or scary. Or is there a group of SENSUOUS EXPERIENCES—things heard, smelled, tasted, touched, and seen. Looking at your map, you may find a cluster of numbers in SOME IMPORTANT AREA OR PLACE.

Before writing your draft, if it's a single "big" item that interests you, asterisk its number. If it's a group of (maybe three to five) images that somehow fit together, asterisk *them*. Or simply asterisk those items you like best; a pattern will probably emerge from your work.

If possible, find Someone to show your map to. Read aloud your asterisked items. Then tell even more than you've written.

If Someone has a map too, ask to see it and to hear her/his items.

Step 4.   On a sheet of paper write the working title, "Neighborhood." Select an asterisked item that might be good to begin with and work for a strong or musical phrase to begin stanza 1. Our idea is that you will use this phrase, or something like it, to begin each stanza or chunk.

Here are three beginnings for poems based mainly on *a single item*. Our asterisked item read: "Billy Finnegan ran away, last day of school, and actually got lost in Burns Park. We all searched for him."

We thought "a strong, musical beginning" might be:
    "Finnegan's gone. . . ."

Here are two others we culled from asterisked items:
    "Apple pies, rhubarb, mince meat and peach" (a "pie day" for kids).
    "That day our 'hood turned red" (a neighborhood fire).

Here are three more beginnings, these based on *patterns of items*:
    "We played our games beyond the fence . . ."
    "I loved four boys with sunshine smiles . . ."
    Ma had these rules. "Now hear," she said . . .

If you don't find a pattern of items, try some general phrase:
    At Vinewood and Fourth . . .
    That was the place . . .
    Things I remember . . .

Another way to get a beginning phrase is to ask yourself a question *based* on an item on our List. Ask *"What did you do back then?"*

You answer: *Where no one could see me I'd climb* . . .
    (Following stanzas might begin,
    "Where no one could hear me . . ."
    and "Where no one could touch me . . .")

Ask *"Where were the dangerous places?"*

    "Not near the creek," Father said

(Following stanzas might begin,
    "Not in the street . . ." and
    "Not in that house . . .")

Ask *"Where could you collect things?"*

    We found two flattened pennies near the tracks . . .

Here are other refrain lines we like:

> Sixty-five North Cretin Street . . .
> "Ready or not," Martha called . . .
> Tom Jacobs lived there, him and his gang . . .

(and)   Cross Mayhews' yard, into the woods

A refrain is usually a repeated line or phrase. As repetitions or echoes in music and art are often powerful, they can work magic in poetry too. Although we're suggesting here that you begin stanzas with them, REFRAINS CAN APPEAR OTHER PLACES AS WELL—at the ends of stanzas, for example. It's also fun to set up a pattern of refrains and then *change individual refrains in* some artful way. Experiment, remembering to read aloud, inviting your ear to tell you what's good.

Step 5.   With the working title ("Neighborhood") and a draft of a beginning phrase, you're ready to *transform your asterisked items from ordinary language into "poetry language."* There are many ways of making this transformation. For example, replacing fuzzy inexact words with sharp, accurate ones; finding a concrete image "to stand for" an idea or feeling; looking for "the right place" to end each line; listening for the sounds of key words to echo with a full or partial rhyme, *et cetera.*

We're going to focus on one way that gets right to the heart of differences between poetry and prose: compressed language. Poetry tends to be shorter, more compact than prose. Poetry is said to be "DISTILLED"—ALL "EXCESS WORDS" BOILED OUT OF IT. Poetry tends to cut out (unwanted) repetitions of words or ideas. It tends to use images (e.g., "The child waddled" or "Our licorice rope of a street") for longer, more literal descriptions (e.g., "The chubby child walked heavily, like a duck or a goose" or "The street, narrow and black, was ours"). Poetry tends to cut out "little words," leaving nouns and verbs and (less often) adjectives and adverbs. ("The house was set a little way into the woods" becomes "Just inside the woods, that house.")

You'll find other ways of cutting. And once you learn to cut to something sharp and good, you'll find good ways of adding. But for now . . . Cut your twenty-plus word items by as much as you can. Cut to the point where what's left is the meat—the best, most vivid part. Specifically, try to *cut each item to fifteen words or fewer.*

As you look for ways to cut to fifteen or fewer words, you'll be paying attention to the language in "a poetry way."

Here's one of our examples from above, cut to size:

(Old)	(New)
The sun rose over the pines	Sun through the pines
in Billy Atwater's big yard. I had	in Billy's yard, me squinting

to squint into it those mornings   with each catch. (12 words)
Billy and I played catch. (24 words)

Good! We cut it in half! And it looks and sounds OK. Here's a complete poem we've squeezed pretty hard.

Text 39   **Pineos' Porch**

Something's gone
from Pineos' porch. I see
when Billy and I
go to play ball at Groveland Park.

We take turns being Dizzy Dean.
Walking home I check out
Pineos' porch. Then
when Ma sends me to buy

smokes at A&P, I walk
way out of my way, up Oak.
Something's sure missing
from Pineos'. I wonder

did it use to rock
up and back, half in shade,
cackle *Hello! you boy!*
when I walked by?

Step 6.   Work away, finishing a first draft. Then work it over and *enter a revised draft into your notebook.* Don't wait until Some Other Responsibility lands on you with all four feet.
Here's another neighborhood we know.

Text 40   **ONE TIME**

When evening had flowed between houses
and paused on the schoolground, I met
Hilary's blind little sister following
the gray smooth railing still warm from the sun
with her hand; and she stood by the edge
holding her face upward waiting
while the last light found her cheek
and her hair, and then on over the trees.

You could hear the great sprinkler arm
of water find and then leave the pavement,
and pigeons telling each other their dreams
or the dreams they would have. We were
deep in the well of shadow by then, and I
held out my hand, saying, "Tina, it's me—
Hilary says I should tell you it's dark,
and, oh, Tina, it is. Together now—"

And I reached, our hands touched,
and we found our way home.

Poems in Response

First Fizzed

70's blaring rock music,
car-washing sun
(sizzle)
days from next door.
On other street:
pony with white mane
(used to live)
there.
Child-planned "Fun Day;"
sign announcing
falls and is forgotten
with once-stapled purple Fizz candy I have
never tasted
(until now)
and want to.
I want to know the
Fizz.
Fizzing sun, sizzles my eyes and
hot skin.
A
(now falsely)
drawn-out fizzle
of life between too-pregnant intervals
flickering and fizzling on and off
with
awareness.
Fizzle, sizzle, sissle
Sssssssssssssssss.
ssssnake in the grass over by that house
People shoot you??
someone says
Shoot themselves?
But I am too small to understand rumors
let alone
Mortality.
All I know is that I want that
Fizz.

—Megan Grumbling

My House glowed,
waiting . . .
supper, Mom, Dad,
the world, it seemed
waiting there for me.

sitting on the steps,
sharing animal crackers
with my shaggy, brown-eyed shadow.
He danced, tail wagging,
eyes darting— to the box. to me.
He always got the last one.

Running barefoot in summer,
arms outstretched hugging the afternoon.
I sang made-up songs,
told of places I'd never seen,
people I'd never met.

Indian summer.
Dust rose from gravel roads.
And I watched
sunset blazing through flame-kissed trees

Making snow angels, Mom, Dad, and I.
Coldness and laughter burned
in our lungs
as snowballs flew.

Afternoons at Stacy Harles' house.
Warm, wonderful, craziness.
Someone always coming or going.
The eight of them laughing.

We spent those days, Stacy and I,
Among trees, sunshine, smiles
and dragons, unicorns, witches, fairies.
in the Enchanted Lands of my backyard.

My house glowed,
waiting . . .
supper, Mom, Dad,
the world, it seemed
waiting there for me.

—Erin Merz

TIME MOVED QUICKLY ON

As I walked around the block, time moved quickly on . . .

    I saw myself buying popsicles from
the ice-cream man on the bike, ringing his bell,
herding his flocks.
    I saw myself skipping down the sidewalk
in a mist of rain, my hair matted on my forehead,
my cheeks pink.

As I walked around the block, time moved quickly on . . .

    I saw Mrs. McCormick in her backyard with
Peaches nipping at her heels.
    I saw Mr. Strand asking me where he should
plant the petunias and Mrs. Strand
playing with her roses.

As I walked around the block, time moved quickly on . . .

    I saw the house I KNEW people lived in
(but never saw) and
    the Herb's gypsy beads tinkling against a dark
window on a breathless Halloween night.

As I walked around the block, time moved quickly on . . .

    The people with the pond shooed me away
from the goldfish that so raptly held my attentions
    and Somebody's cranky cocker spaniel
barked incessantly at every irregular noise.

As I walked around the block, time moved quickly on . . .

    I saw myself sitting on my swing,
feet digging ruts in the green lawn.
    My eyes spilling tears for my
absent friends who left me here to

walk around the block as time moved quickly on.

—Lena James

The sun rose over the hill by the bus stop
And on the way there I'd walk
Up the path Mom said had poison ivy
So I was climbing into the dawn.

The Bateman's white mutt, Kelly, was
Always let loose and one day jumped
On me, putting muddy paws all over

My new white jeans. The Lochirco's
Dog was old and crippled but she had
Kind brown eyes and a soft pink tongue.

Out front was the road, a silvery wet
River in the rain. The back was a
Wild riot of the Tremallo's forsythias
Every spring. Alone, I'd creep to the
Hide-out, woods in the side yard
And pretend to be Maid Marian or
Robin Hood. Sometimes my brother
and I would play at being Vikings.

But my favorite times were when
Anthony and Michael came over to play
Football. Anthony and I raced and
I was always faster. When their dad
Left with some other woman, I pitied
them but never understood their pain.

When they first moved in across the street
Anthony came one night to say hello and
Asked if we could play after dinner.
But there were things I couldn't ask
About his life so I just threw
Snowballs at him and showed him
How peeled birch bark smells like root beer,
Hoping he'd understand what I meant to say.

—Arielle J. Siebert

Tomboy Days

We sneaked through the woods,
reed swords at our sides.
The oak tree was our castle,
the creek, our moat.

We sailed through the water,
reed swords at our sides.
The row boat was our pirate ship,
the tackle box, our loot.

We sloshed through the woods,
reed swords at our sides.
The cattails were our torches,
the marsh, the new world.

—Nancy Ryan

Finnegan's Alley

Meet me at midnight
near Finnegan's Alley
We'll stand in the cold
and pretend to be smoking.

Meet me at midnight
don't dilly, don't dally
We'll race down the concrete
until noses are raw, our hearts pounding.

Meet me at midnight
where the icicles are
We'll lick them with warm tongues
until they melt in our mittens.

Meet me at midnight
between the parked cars
in the lot behind the tavern: we'll
snowball old men.

Meet me at midnight
my old-fashioned friend
We'll sneak out at midnight
then back in again.

—Krista Wark

Running Away

Looking out for myself,
I ran away
One night when a trace of snow
Hid footprints in the icy crust
On sidewalks and in yards.

Looking out for myself,
Angry at something lost from memory now,
I stood like a revolutionary awaiting the bullets,
stood against our neighbor's maple where he, an old hunter,
nailed rabbits for skinning.
The night was damp and still.

Looking out for myself,
I ducked past our kitchen lights,
square and yellow on the snow. My mother and sisters,
all in aprons, were finishing dishes.
I scraped between the two spruces
guarding our dining room windows.

Looking in at my family,
I could see the clang and clink of pans and dishes,
see the conversations, see my brother and father
reading the newspaper like a map, sports then comics.

Looking out for myself,
I had announced I was leaving, escaping.
Looking in at my family, I could see
They were not coming to search.
Looking in at my family,
I backed through the arms of the spruces
And walked to the empty corner lot
Where we played baseball and football: local wars.
A huge oak tree near one endzone, near home plate,
Had a hole that shrunk each year.
I threw a chunk of snow at it: low and wide.

Looking out for myself,
Looking in at my family,
I spent my rebellion on the still stars and frozen air,
And entered the back door
As if I'd just returned from another day of fourth grade.

Years later my father admitted
They had noticed by the light of the dining room
My red wool cap, part of my winter uniform,
Gliding past the window sills as I stood
Against the dark spruces
Looking in at my family,
Looking out for myself.

—Randall Heeres

Neighborhood

I am from Wickom Avenue
where Mr. and Mrs. Gallagher
laughed and drank beer, Buzzy
palled with me, Marty
fought all comers, and little Dave
was on his way to pro ball.

I am from Wickom Avenue
where Mr. Alonzo frowned, Lillian
covering her living room with plastic, Dennis
remained outcast, trying too hard to be a friend.

I am from Wickom Avenue
where my mother cleaned house, my father
read and disappeared into his basement shop, my brother
and sister left before I knew, and I
just played.

I am from Wickom Avenue,
where my father died in the hall, Mr. Gal
choked to death on beer vomit, alone
in bed, Marty and Bogey
next door formed a drug ring, and my brother
returned from Vietnam with
a wife, a drug habit, and nightmares.

I am from Wickom Avenue,
the Cape Cod homes and backyards,
the basements and the woods, the grown-ups,
the older boys, Buzzy, and the ghosts
in these lines.

—Bob Coleman

Finding Palfrey Hill

Climbing Palfrey Hill
    Home from a first grade day
        Tom's wobbly cardboard box held
            Fluffy the kitten.

Climbing Palfrey Hill
    Home from his city job
        Pop's shiny black Ford held
            Comic books, limburger cheese.

Climbing Palfrey Hill
    Chanting his weekly refrain
        The ragman's dent-riddled truck held
            "R - a - a - a - g - s."

Climbing Palfrey Hill
    Back from Lauricella's Spa
        Mama's lumpy string bag held
            Pickles, butter in a golden slab, jumbo eggs.

Climbing Palfrey Hill
    Up from Watertown Square
        Cushman's Bakery truck held
            Shelves of cellophaned sweetness.

Climbing Palfrey Hill
  Screeching to stop in the dust
    My balloon-tired, red two-wheeler held—
    I never knew it then—
      Childhood.

—Sheila G. Murphy

Interlude

Reference Points for Your Life

Writing hardly gets any richer than it does when you range outward into your community and respond to actual things there. For instance, the play "Our Town" sustains itself on the momentum of remembered places, people, and events—you have probably experienced that play, its dreamlike and yet actual evoking of someone's home place.

That resonance in your own life can sustain your writing. Whatever your neighborhood, it provides endless riches for the people in it—hence the care in making a map and filling it with what counts. The result of such inventories is a collection of bright pieces that can be turned over like chips of paint and made into meaningful pictures.

With these arrangements of what everyone knows, you range out into original material; for no one else relates exactly as you do. Your senses bring an always-new world, fixed and then changed by the magic of your writing.

Dialogue Poems

Introduction

As do movies, novels, stories, plays and many TV shows, poems have characters in them. And—ready?—characters talk. The dialogue poem focuses on characters' talk.

But first, to complicate things for a moment . . .

Many poems seem to have a voice or speaker who "tells" the poem. And often this teller is given the name "I."

Who is "I"? It's inviting (but not fully useful) to answer that question by saying, "Well, dummy, the 'I' of the poem is the poet."

Hmmm. We read the beginning of this Emily Dickinson poem . . .

> I died for beauty, but was scarce
> Adjusted in the tomb,
> When one who died for truth was lain
> In an adjoining room.

What are we to think? Here's Emily ("I") writing shortly after her death?

Better than believing "I" to be Emily, think of "I" as a character in a "made-up thing"—like a story or play. Think of "I" as the "teller" of the poem. A "character" (or "persona"). Granted, this "teller" may have close ties to the author; in fact, some poems seem to come straight from the poet's actual life. But if we look at a poem as "a fiction" or "drama" we will be ahead of readers who think of it as "true document" or "testimony." We know Emily wrote her poem when she was living and well. Emily's "I" isn't (altogether) she herself. We focus here on **talk** because it makes poems so darned convincing.

Dialogue Poem Steps

Step 1.

Text 41

Read this poem consisting exclusively of a title plus talk.

Conoco Sam

"Fill it up, regular."
　　"Sure thing. My eyes are bad."
"Could I fill my canteen?"
　　"Sure thing. Got maybe a year of
　　sight left."
"Windshield's pretty bad, isn't it?"
　　"Yep. Good thing cows don't fly—
　　but I could see *them*."
"Looks like rain."

"Sure does. Feels like it too."
"You didn't give me enough change."
"Damn! Can't see a thing any more."

—Jim Heynen

Except for the title, the entire poem is dialogue. Although one speaker's words are indented, both speakers seem to be named "I." Who's who, here? How are they different, these two "I's"? Especially, what sort of person is Sam?

Notice that each piece of talk is enclosed in quotes. What clues are there on *where* and *when* the poem takes place?

Step 2.   Here's a similar kind of dialogue to read and think about.

Text 42   **Two Friends**

I have something to tell you.
I'm listening.
I'm dying.
I'm sorry to hear.
I'm growing old.   (5)
It's terrible.
It is, I thought you should know.
Of course and I'm sorry. Keep in touch.
I will and you too.
And let know what's new.   (10)
Certainly, though it can't be much.
And stay well.
And you too.
And go slow.
And you too.   (15)

—David Ignatow

Look Ma: No quotes. No indentations. Still, we have no trouble figuring out where each speaker starts and stops. That each line of the poem is "talk" from a single speaker helps make things clear. And as with "Conoco Sam," except for the title, the entire poem is dialogue. Moreover, both characters are named "I."

But in "Two Friends" the topic of conversation gets pretty heavy. What do you read "between the lines"? Is the first speaker more interested in *telling* than the second speaker is in *listening*? How good a friend to speaker 1 is speaker 2?

What are your guesses as to "where" this poem takes place? What are the ages and sexes of the two speakers? What's your evidence?

Step 3.   *Using either "Conoco Sam" or "Two Friends" as your model,* and giving credit to the one you choose, **draft a dialogue poem** made up *exclusively* of title plus talk. You'll need two speakers.

(Hint: Get your characters in mind before you have them talk. Is one speaker like you? Younger? Older? Sweeter? Meaner? Or is it some *thing* that in real life can't talk—e.g., the wind, the clock on the wall. And what about speaker #2?)

Use *no* speaker tags (such as *she said.*) Use *no* narrations/descriptions (such as *They met at the top of the hill. Jill said . . .*)

As for length, make your poem at least as long as "Conoco Sam"—five "exchanges" between speakers. Each character speaks five times.

One thing more: Whether you imitate the light-heartedness of "Conoco Sam" or the seriousness of "Two Friends" (or take an altogether different attitude), have your poem begin *"in medias res."*

(*Yeah, sure,* you say. *In MAY-dee-us RACE.*)

Remember? Latin for "in the middle of things." For example, "Conoco Sam" might have begun with the driver of the car waking up, taking a shower, feeding her/his cat, starting the engine, driving to Conoco Sam's, rolling down the window . . .

It *could* have begun like that. It didn't. It did something better. It began *in medias res.*

Got it? The poem begins smack in the middle of the scene: "Fill it up, regular." And so with "Two Friends." Imagine for a moment all the action that happened before the first speaker says, "I have something to tell you." Again, *in medias res.*

Step 4.   Usually, dialogue poems have both *talk* and *narration/description.* There is a narrator/speaker who tells the poem, plus characters who speak dialogue. For example:

Text 43   **Shopping**

They met
near pickles
in A & P

He said
Do you know where   (5)
rutabagas are

She saw
the lone artichoke
in his cart. I can
show you the way   (10)

Between zucchini
and cherry tomatoes
they found it
It looks good
he said. He was   (15)
looking at

her eyes
playful as kittens:
I've never tried it

Let me fix you   (20)
some Sunday
he said.

—Dorothy Schieber Miller

In lines 1–3, the *narrator/"teller"* describes the scene: "They met /
near pickles / in A & P." Then in lines 5–6 one character says: "Do
you know where / rutabagas are." Before the other character re-
sponds, the narrator moves (lines 7–9) toward her consciousness, or
point-of-view: "She saw / the lone artichoke . . ."

So, in "Shopping," a narrator "tells the poem" and two characters speak. Because the poet ignores quotation marks and other
punctuation, there are brief (pleasant?) puzzles as to who's speaking.
Now listen: *Most* poets know how to punctuate, but they're driven to
get "clutter" out of their poems—anything that isn't absolutely
necessary. Then, to help readers adjust for missing quotes, indents,
and speaker tags, they provide other clues. In "Shopping" the stanza
changes with each new speaker: Stanza one is the narrator speaking,
two (mainly) the male character, *et cetera*.

Sometimes the narrator who tells the poem also talks in it.

Step 5.

Text 44

PLUS

"Lately I've been eating a lot of pork.
Plus I eat too many eggs and things,"
this guy said to me in the doc's office.
"I pour on the salt. I drink twenty cups
of coffee every day. I smoke.   (5)
I'm having trouble with my breathing."
Then he lowered his eyes.
"Plus, I don't always clear off the table
when I'm through eating. I forget.
I just get up; and walk away.   (10)
Goodbye until the next time, brother.
Mister, what do you think's happening to me?"
He was describing my own symptoms to a T.
I said, "What do you think's happening?
You're losing your marbles. And then   (15)
you're going to die. Or vice versa.
What about sweets? Are you partial
to cinnamon rolls and ice cream?"
"Plus, I crave all that," he said.
By this time we were at a place called Friendly's.   (20)
We looked at menus and went on talking.
Dinner music played from a radio

in the kitchen. It was our song, see.
It was our table.

—Raymond Carver

The "other character" is talking as the poem gets under way "in the middle of things." The narrator ("I") "tells" line 3 ("this guy said to me . . .") and again in line 7 ("Then lowered his eyes.") But "I" really gets more fully into the poem in line 13: He "tells," then talks. From "I said" on, "I" pretty much dominates the poem in "talking" and in "telling."

Step 6.   *Draft a DIALOGUE poem with a narrator.* You'll need someone to "tell" the poem. Below is an example where that telling character is "I"; he/she participates in the dialogue. (Thus the example is more like "Plus" than "Shopping.") "I" says . . .

> I found two soft mice
> curled like beans in the cold
> corner of the barn.

Then "I" speaks:

> *[I found two soft mice*
> *curled like beans in the cold*
> *corner of the barn.]*
> "Finny!" I yelled. "Come see."

Then a second character [Finny] speaks:

> *["Finny!" I yelled. "Come see."]*
> Finny's voice broke like stone.
> "You're the lucky twin.
> You find everything."

Whether your narrator is "silent" or participates in the DIALOGUE, work for four or more exchanges between speakers. Decide whether to use quotation marks and other punctuation. If you leave out that "clutter," arrange things so that it's clear to the reader who's speaking where. Remember, begin *in medias res.*

Step 7.   Of your two drafts (the one with a narrator, the one without), *choose the one you prefer and urge it into a second draft.* Read aloud as you work, hearing the voices. Do they "make the sounds" of the characters you have in mind? If there's too little difference between characters, rework the poem so as to sharpen them—making one male, one female; or one young, one old; or one innocent, the other not; or one human, the other not. . . . Each speaker deserves her/his own voice.
        Enter this revision into your notebook.
        But hey! Your poem is mainly talk. Wouldn't it first be nice to have Someone read one speaker's words aloud as you read the rest?
        Sure.

HOLIDAY HOME

Good to see you, Ma.
I feel terrible.
You're looking good.
My ear's been feeling terrible.
Your dress is awfully pretty—and your hair . . .
Listen to the moaning across the hall.
I notice they've redecorated the hall. Pretty.
She's crazy as a loon. Moans all the time.
The nurses are friendly.
Listen to her holler, Help. Can't hear myself think.
Several patients waved to me from their wheel chairs. Friendly.
You don't know what it's like living in a place like this.
Your room is bright and airy.
There's nobody to talk to here.
The nurses seem friendly.
Everybody's crazy or deaf or moaning or crippled.
Does the priest still say Mass every week?
My ear has pus running out of it.
I hear the chaplain came to see you.
It was the bishop.
I hear it was the priest. He's a nice guy.
He wore a miter.
Priests don't wear miters.
He carried a crozier. He looked like the statue of St. Patrick.
Are you sure it was the bishop?
He forgave all the sins I ever committed.
That's good.
And he forgave all the sins I will ever commit . . .
That's even better.
For the rest of my life.
Good deal! Ma, I have to go now. 'Bye now.
Thanks for coming, Son.
Be seeing you.
When will you come again?
As soon as I can.
Come soon. You always cheer me up.

—James S. Mullican

Reflections

"The food could make you drop dead."
    "But playing with it was fun."
"'No TV,' the counselors said."
    "So we went to the track to run."
"My teacher was crazy."
    "Ours was really great."
"The weather was <u>so</u> hazy."
    "Think of all the <u>junk</u> we ate!"
"The beach was really awesome."
    "'Specially when the waves were high."
"I've got pictures—wanna see 'em?"
    "Oh, you have some? So do I!"
"I didn't think I'd miss it there."
    "I really wasn't sure."
"But now I know that I do care."
    "I'm going back next year."

                                —Elizabeth Dorr

Motherhood

What's that?
    A butterfly.
Why?
    I don't know.
Why?
    It's just what they're called.
Why?
    Someone a long time ago decided it was a good name.
Why?
    I don't know.
Why?
    Because I don't know everything.
Why?
    Because no one knows everything.
Why?
    I don't know.
What's that?
    A flower.
Why?

                                —Sheila R. Hawkins

Okay, it's five nine two, three six eight seven.
Five nine two, three six eight seven?
Yeah . . . and it's Andrea.
How old are you?
Sixteen.
Oh!
How old are you?
Fourteen.
Oh. What's your name?
You'll find out.
Seriously, what's your name?
You'll find out.
No, seriously, tell me.
You'll find out.
Okay.
I'll call you.

—Andrea Siegrist

Katie's Good-Bye

"Can I come?"
No—you're too . . .
"Why?"

You're only four.
"I'm a big girl, I'll be good."
I don't have space.
"Why?"

It's a small room . . .
"I'm little, I'll be good, can I come pleeease?"
No—your mom and dad will . . .
"Why?"

Your parents will miss you.
"Mommy and daddy fight, you won't fight. Can I . . . ?"
No—it's all the way in . . .
"Why?"

It's far away.
"If I can't come to college, I don't love you anymore!"

But I will always love you, Katie. Good-Bye.

—Tracy Phillips

Interlude

Many Voices

Talking it over is a way to decide, when two or more people are planning. Each voice has its own angle, and when voices converge the result is likely to be richer than with the ideas of just one.

And strangely, even when just one does the thinking, as in a written piece of dialogue, the form of the writing seems to elicit extra richness. Maybe a really rich thinker keeps voices going back and forth—inside the self—to increase the chances for insight.

A teller needs a listener, and reactions from that listener. At least, a teller should be ready for reactions, and be alerted to new angles as perceived by someone else.

The fun of it, in writing dialogue, is that you can set up both parts of the conversation, guiding the progress just the way you want it. Dialogue can energize your writing.

Imitation 3

Introduction

Some people properly connect the word *litanies* with religious services. But the litanies we have in mind are more those with repetitions and chant-like qualities. Here's an example that has repetitions, probably could be chanted, and may also connect vaguely (if not seriously) with some religious meaning of litany.

Text 45

Forgive

Forgive the far cast to my eye
   the way it closes to praise.
Forgive breaths I've taken
   from lungs of the poor.
Forgive the smile held back. (5)
Forgive my not calling Jack
   whose mind has cracked,
& forgive times I dreamt unneeded dreams.
Forgive the bitter whine to my shout.
Forgive money spent, but more (10)
Forgive all money saved.
Forgive my ears their theft of music
   my nose the smells inhaled.
Forgive sights I've kept as my own.
Forgive pride and sloth, forgive (15)
   not forgiving. Forgive even hope.

What makes something **chant-like** is hard to say, although probably we could agree on a few songs and football cheers as chants. What's **repetitious** is easier to define. The obvious repetition above is the word *forgive*. What the speaker wants forgiven sometimes seems predictable and sometimes surprising.

Repetition itself is a key characteristic of poetry. For example, *line-end rhymes* in a rhyming poem make a pattern of repeated sounds. So do other kinds of rhyme—"assonance" (a repetition of vowel sounds) and "consonance" (a repetition of consonant sounds).

Rhythms repeat, too, repeating patterns of accented and unaccented syllables (for example, u/ u/ u/ allowing a line to be described as "iambic"), and patterns of lines in stanzas that can be called, for example, couplets or quatrains.

Litany Poem Steps

Step 1.
Text 46

Read this saucy poem with its obvious repetitions:

Ode on a Big Leg Woman

When I watch Paula Abdul
I feel like eating a thick steak.
I feel like taking a lap.
I feel like lifting something heavy and renewing
    my subscription to <u>Muscle and Fitness.</u>
I feel like getting tattooed.
I feel like watching football on Monday night.
I feel like digging a dry well.
I feel like changing my oil.
I feel like drinking a sixpack.
I feel like eating a bucket of chicken
    and getting all greased up.
I feel like breaking commandments 3, 5, 7, and 11.
I feel like doing rude things.

—Jeff Stockton

Step 2.

Copy-change a draft of "Ode . . ." Imitate these three specific aspects:

(a) a title *like* "Ode . . . ," using a different word from "ode" (such as "poem," "elegy," "song," "lyric," "ballad," or "chant");

(b) a first line beginning with "when"—or a different word you prefer—that sets up a "premise" or situation; and

(c) at least ten lines beginning **not** with "I feel like" but with similar language. So far as is possible and comfortable, imitate Stockton's light-hearted, sassy/sexy tone.

When finished with your copy-change, credit Stockton's poem.

For example, *"After reading Jeff Stockton's 'Ode . . .'"*

Step 3.

The two litanies following have quite different "tones." Read both aloud, perhaps several times each, and **draft a copy-change of the one that attracts you more.** Try to find a good substitute for the word "fear" in imitating the Carver poem, and/or a different activity from "painting" in imitating Swenson.

Text 47

Fear

Fear of seeing a police car pull into the drive.
Fear of falling asleep at night.
Fear of not falling asleep.
Fear of the past rising up.
Fear of the present taking flight.
Fear of the telephone that rings in the dead of night.

Fear of electrical storms.
Fear of the cleaning woman who has a spot on her cheek!
Fear of dogs I've been told won't bite.
Fear of anxiety!
Fear of having to identify the body of a dead friend.
Fear of running out of money.
Fear of having too much, though people will not believe this.
Fear of psychological profiles.
Fear of being late and fear of arriving before anyone else.
Fear of my children's handwriting on envelopes.
Fear they'll die before I do, and I'll feel guilty.
Fear of having to live with my mother in her old age, and mine.
Fear of confusion.
Fear this day will end on an unhappy note.
Fear of waking up to find you gone.
Fear of not loving and fear of not loving enough.
Fear that what I love will prove lethal to those I love.
Fear of death.
Fear of living too long.
Fear of death.
    I've said that.

—Raymond Carver

Text 48

Painting the Gate

I painted the mailbox. That was fun.
I painted it postal blue.
Then I painted the gate.
I painted a spider that got on the gate.
I painted his mate.
I painted the ivy around the gate.
Some stones I painted blue,
and part of the cat as he rubbed by.
I painted my hair. I painted my shoe.
I painted the slats, both front and back,
all their beveled edges, too.
I painted the numbers on the gate—
I shouldn't have, but it was too late.
I painted the posts, each side and top,
I painted the hinges, the handle, the lock,
several ants and a moth asleep in a crack.
At last I was through.
I'd painted the gate
shut, me out, with both hands dark blue,
as well as my nose, which
early on, because of a sudden itch,
got painted. But wait!
I had painted the gate.

—May Swenson

Once you've completed a draft of your copy-change, give credit to the original in some appropriate way.

Step 4. This next model poem may seem simple, compared to the poems above. Believe us, it isn't. It asks you to create specific images and to make metaphors.

Text 49

Dreams

Hold fast to dreams
For if dreams die
Life is a broken-winged bird
That cannot fly.

Hold fast to dreams
For if dreams go
Life is a barren field
Frozen with snow.

—Langston Hughes

Step 5. **Copy-change a draft** of "Dreams."

First jot down three or four ideas for titles that imitate both the specific "advice" ("Hold fast") and the general subject ("dreams").

Repeat your title as the first line of your poem. Start your second line with "for," or some word like that. Imitate the metaphor of the third line: it takes the abstract word "life" and says that it is something specific and concrete—"a broken-winged bird / That cannot fly." Note that it doesn't say "life" is **like** "a broken-winged bird." Life simply **is.**

Imitate the second stanza, too. Text 49 will remind you how.

Interlude

Words in a Ritual Way

We are all used to leader-response patterns, as in church, or maybe in cheerleader chants and yells. The pattern lends itself to fast imitation, substituting your own content in the established form.

These back-forth, leader-to-audience, practices can merge into insistent one-voice patterns too. The repetitions build up into quite an effective experience; the reader or hearer has expectations after the pattern gets established, and meeting those expectations (or sometimes deviating purposefully) is the trick.

Easy? Yes, but also sometimes powerful, as cheerleaders know, as leaders on public occasions demonstrate again and again.

Confession Poems

Introduction

OK, 'fess up. Time to come clean. Divulge your own character flaws. Reveal those suspicions you've had about Aunt Letty. Confess secrets nobody knows. Share with Teacher your true feelings about adverbs.

"Confession is good for the soul," they say.

But probably you shouldn't tell *everything.* At least, don't tell US everything. *There are things we don't want to hear.* Your ugliest thoughts might embarrass us. Something mean might hurt. So the **confession poem** brings with it the need to draw that line between what should go public and what should stay private.

That's sometimes a hard line to draw. Most good poems "take risks." Many skirt the edges of privacy. Yet you have secrets that probably should remain secret. If you make Secret X public, it'll embarrass you and the person who hears it. If you tell Secret Z, someone will be hurt. So as a goal for this exercise, try to **approach serious topics with humor, with distance, and with taste.** Try to get "close to the bone" but not bite into it. Stop short of revealing thoughts that could embarrass or hurt. Here's a poem that seems to do that.

Text 50

My Self

I choose to keep my self
to me, for way down deep
me be too fine to share
with old just anybody there.

When self go out at night   (5)
to do a little stroll
the face old self put on
be blank, all clues be off

an self wear hair to match
the face, the face that match   (10)
the clothes, the nowhere clothes
that no old anybody knows.

Only bones betray my self
an I keep my bones covered.
Me, the boss of self's old bones.   (15)
Right now I showin no one.

"My Self" seems to be about "I's" wanting to keep "self" private. So "I" puts on a face (1. 7), hair (1. 9), and clothes (1. 11) to "mask" the real self (ll. 13–16). "I's" in charge, and "Right now [she/he's] showin no one."

What sort of person is "I"? How do you read "too fine" (1. 3)? What does line 5 seem to mean? (What's your proof?) What if the poet had put this "epigraph" under the title: "To Mother, who's always prying"?

One thing more about "My Self." We talked above about "I's" wanting to keep 'self' private." As if "I" were some character. Who is this "I"?

Of course you can say that "I" is the poet talking from personal experience. "I" is the poet's name for her/himself in the poem. But remember, *we instead see "I" as a persona or character created by the poet*, and see the poem as a product of imagination. Sure, there's a connection between the poet's experience and the feeling of the poem. But the experience could be someone's other than the poet's, or could have been imagined by the poet.

Think of "I" as a (persona) character when you read and write poems.

People seem fascinated by "inside stories." When it comes to "gossip" from queens and presidents, rock stars and local celebrities, we can't get enough. Even the evening news brings more violence, scandal, and deceit than kind acts and good. Is there more evil than good in the world?

We don't think so. We think that most of us, in our daily lives, do more "good" than "bad"—help people more than we exploit them; are friendly and good-natured more than unfriendly and surly. *Not that we're perfect.*

It's "little secrets" we're after in "the confession poem." Not your deepest secrets—your worst quirks and naughtinesses. We want those naughty little ones that can be brought out into sunlight! Things we'll be glad to hear about, not embarrassed by.

SO LET US CONFESS A FEW THINGS. Two things WE have done are to lie and to steal. (Oooh! We want to soften those words, *lie* and *steal*. We want to explain how the lie was just a *little* lie, one to save time.) It was like . . .

> *"Son," Mother asked, "did you come straight home from school?"*
> *"Yes ma'am," we said.*
> *If we told the truth, see, that Pat Justice bought a Twinkie at the 7-Eleven and shared it—Pat always had money—and then we had to go into Pat's father's Marathon Station to wash our sticky hands, and while we were there, Mr. Justice showed us piston rods he'd pulled out of an old Buick, and that got our hands all dirty again . . . if we told all that, we'd be left out of kick ball in Tom Feinberg's backyard.*

Just a tiny lie. BUT A LIE!

As for stealing, we didn't actually *steal*, as in hold up a bank and take money. What we did can hardly be called stealing. All we did was . . .

> *keep that nice ballpoint somebody left in our desk in history class; and that other day Old Eagle-eye Jones, the checkout person, failed to notice **both** ice cream bars on our lunch tray, we didn't say anything; and then that motel towel we took to clean up the spill in our car, we always meant to take it back.*

You wouldn't call those examples *stealing*, would you? YUP!

Confession Poem Steps

Step 1.

Starting with words (like) "Once I . . ." write 35–50 words about a lie you've told. Use names (or made-up ones—more lies!) and specifics. Say what the lie was, why you told it, and what the consequences were, if any. It's OK to invent the whole thing. Label this **Warm-up A.** Either prose or poem-like is OK. Write the number of words at the end.

Then *starting with words like "And once I . . ."* write 35–50 words about something you "stole" (took without permission, borrowed and forgot to return). Say what you took, why you took it, and what were the consequences. Label this **Warm-up B.** Either prose or poetry. Put the number of words at the end.

(Remember, Angel: if you've *never* lied nor stolen invent **A** and **B.**)

Step 2.

Is it their frailties that make people interesting? Or their virtues? Or a mix? We're using the word *frailties* to move from those uneasy behaviors of lying and stealing to lesser crimes. FROM THE LIST BELOW, CHOOSE TWO that connect (or that you're willing to imagine things about):

> **Frailties list.**
>
> taking more than your share
>
> pretending to be sick
>
> blaming someone else for something you did
>
> saying something mean
>
> being thoughtless/cruel to animals
>
> breaking a promise
>
> repeating (or making up) gossip

Starting with language like *"Another time . . ."* or *"I also . . ."* or *"Although I didn't mean . . . ,"* write up—in 35–50 words each—the two items you chose. If there's a humorous side, use it. In fact, since these crimes don't deserve the death penalty anyway, maybe you *should* exaggerate. (Exaggerate! Another dang word for *lie*.) In any case, be specific. Label these **Warm-ups C** and **D.** As with **A** and **B,** jot down the number of words at the end of each chunk.

Step 3.   Using Warm-ups **A–D** as raw material, *write a two-stanza confession poem. Include parts from all four chunks.* Squeeze two parts together and combine them into **one** stanza.
                Use "Confessions" as a working title.

Step 4.   Ready for some discipline? *Like confession, discipline's good for the soul.* Make *each stanza eight lines long,* and make *each line five to eight words long.* (Thus you're cutting from 70–100 words [the combined length of A and B] to 40–64.) In general, these "formal disciplines" mean that you're cutting your **Warm-up** by *about* one third.

                WHY DO THIS? To force yourself down to the essence of language, to the bones of poem. To cut nonessentials. To find short ways for what you've said long ways. The premise is that short is (often) better than long.

                HOW TO DO THIS CUTTING?

(1) The easiest way is to eliminate not single words or phrases but sentences or parts of sentences. "Save the best and reconnect it."

(2) After you've cut parts, find different words/images to substitute for the ordinary places in your Warm-up version.

(3) Also look for duplications of words or feelings. Cut or combine.

(4) Look at all adjectives and adverbs: cut unless they're pure gold.

(5) Cut the starters we provided earlier.

(6) Cut all connectors that aren't absolutely necessary. Little words, especially. *the, an, but, for, when, since, after, into . . .* Readers of poems know how to "leap" from one image to the next, so look for places where an image can be substituted for a description. Then look for phrases where a single word or shorter version of a phrase can take the place of something longer.

FOR EXAMPLE (from our **Frailties list**) "Blaming someone else . . ."

Ms Cochran had already said	Ms Cochran said, "One word
if I talked once more	more, you're in the hall."
I'd be out in the hall	Nelson roamed those hallway seas
where Vice-Principal Nelson	a killer-sub. "Schultze, Ms C,
cruised the hall like a destroyer	I swear it was Schultze."**[25 words]**
looking for someone to sink.	Later Schultze whapped me
"It was Schultze said that," I said	good. I kicked Lassie's butt.
"I swear, Ms Cochran, it wasn't me."	"Leave me alone, dumb dog."
[C total, 44 words]	[C and D total, 39 words]

We combined Warm-ups C and D (81 words) into one stanza of 39 words, less than half the original count. *Well, hey! Lean and mean.* We cut so many words we have only four words in one line. (So sue us. At least we kept to eight lines!) Now notice *how* we pared from 81 to 39. We saved words by putting Ms Cochran's words into quoted speech. We saved words by substituting *killer-sub* for eight words.

We know. Someone's thinking, "I like the longer version better."

OK. We sort of like it ourselves. But as a rule we favor shorter versions. We like language that requires us to pay close attention in order that we read it well. How's that as a partial definition of poetry—"language that demands that attention be paid"?

And remember, we still have our lean-mean 39-word version. We didn't sink it. Now we can **add** a few words, if we want.

Step 5.   Read these five excerpts from Lowell Jaeger's "Confessions."

Text 51

(E)   I've thrown sticks at stray dogs.
I've ignored the cat
scratching to get in.
Even in rain I've spent
idle hours watching tv, while
not two feet away
philodendrons for lack of
water, gasp and expire.

(F)   Once my tiniest daughter banged
in the backdoor, beaming, her fist
full of wadded five-dollar bill she'd
unearthed on the playground. For it
I swapped the shiny fifty-cent piece
she mingled among her pennies, her
plastic purse jingling with joy.

(G)   I've neglected birthdays
of people who remember mine
First week of December last year
an old friend mailed me a shirt.
I wore it twice, decided it wasn't
for me, folded it, wrapped it, put
it under the tree. "Merry Xmas Brother."

(H)   I once hung that little brother
by the straps of his overalls
on a utility hook nailed into
the garage wall, five feet high.
He giggled helplessly at his
big brother's mischief. I dashed inside
to fetch the Instamatic I'd got
for being nine, wanting to snap
his scrapbook smile. . . .

> (I)   I once swiped a tin of Vienna
> sausages. I crouched low in the aisle
> as if studying percents
> of daily requirements, tore off the lid
> pulled out a wiener and sucked it down.
> I cruised the produce, pocketed
> a nectarine, popped seedless grapes
> into the hopper, fast as my choppers
> could chew. A man in a white, bloody
> apron intercepted me at checkout.

Step 6. Using the working title **"Exposé"** (ex-po-ZAY), *draft a two-stanza poem,* using subjects like those above or ideas of your own.

    As one way of working . . . Model closely on Jaeger's stanzas. Adapt the ideas in Jaeger's stanzas and make your stanzas seven to ten lines long. (Please reread **E.)** If we were using **E** as a model, we might begin:

> I've tried to drown ants with spit.
> I thumped the goldfish bowl
> to make fish dance, and once
> fed them bits of rubber bands I cut
> with scissors I wasn't to use.

Using **F** as a model, we might begin

> The neighbor kid they took out
> Trick and Treating got maximum treats—
> bagfuls of Snickers, Tootsie Rolls
> galore. People gave Jack apples . . .

Notice how in **F** we created a character (Jack). If you wish, create a character and have her/him confess. In any case, use the model stanzas as closely as you wish. Then, however closely you worked with Jaeger's stanzas, **give credit.** Perhaps *"Based on excerpts from Lowell Jaeger's 'Confessions'"* or (more simply) *"In the style of Lowell Jaeger"* will do fine. Good places to give credit are at the top, under the title, or at the bottom. **In your Notebook:** after your own name *enter a good draft* of "Confessions" or "Exposé," whichever you prefer.

Poems in Response

Deals With God

Once I told God,
"Let me win this election,
and I'll never be mean
or cruel again." I promised
to become a modern saint.
When Marilyn Hall won by several votes,
I took pleasure in telling
how she cheated in geometry.

I once promised Him
I'd say the rosary
every night until I died
if only He would make Tommy DeHart
like me. Tommy took me
to the movies, held my hand
and kissed me gently.
Every night for two weeks
I recited the long, long prayer.

—Nona Horsley

Confessions of a Murderer

I broke the handle off a cup
Didn't want Mom to yell
So I put the handle inside it
And hid the whole thing
Behind the potato chips

When my sister was in college
We snagged sugar-packets wherever we went
She managed to filch an ashtray once
And she doesn't even smoke

Sitting beside a pool one day
I noticed a fly in the water
So I helped him out
Then pulled off his wings
And threw him back to see him struggle

—Elizabeth Freimuth

I've carved my sister's
name on the underside
of the family coffee table
which screams at me now
in my own family room.

Once I slipped a handful of
Bazooka bubble gum in my
pocket, and the bulge did
not make it past my mom's or
the grocer's beady eye.

After school my friend and
I were to walk the new girl
home, but we ditched her instead.
The new girl, Shirley Johnson,
went on to be Homecoming Queen.

—Karen N. Reynolds
(In the Style of Lowell Jaeger)

True Confessions

I ran my mom's Saab into an electrical pole and told her that a
   Detroit Edison truck had run into me.
I kept my horse, Pretty Penny, a secret from my husband by paying
   for her with the grocery money.
I picked all the four-leaf clovers from the box of Lucky Charms
   before feeding the rest to my kids.

And I bought a candle shaped like a giant Hershey's Kiss for my
   friend Candy but lit it for myself.
I dressed up like Santa Claus on Halloween and gave milk and sugar
   cookies to the trick-or-treaters.
I locked the cat in the bathroom with a mouse, turned the shower on,
   and went out to lunch.

But I bought a bushel of seashells at an estate sale because someone
   spent a lifetime collecting them.
I chose the snarly kitten with the worms and earmites over the silky
   kitten with the great purr.
I told my mom that I crashed the car, my husband that I have a
   horse, and my kids that there are no lucky charms.

—Nancy Ryan
(Based on "Confessions" by Lowell Jaeger)

Strawberry button slipped so easily
In my pocket. Munsingwear won't mind.
"I found it on the floor." Just like
Dad can't prove I don't
Have a stomach ache, head pains
Sore shoulder, burning fever and
Achy knees. It's definitely
Something serious. I can't go to school.

I better stay home. Watch TV
And get better. Or with
My best friend Kris watch
The boys at the mall. Have to
Be home, suffering acutely
From stomach cramps, sore knees,
Head pains, shoulder aches and high temperature
Before Mom comes home.

—Ann Klein

Exposé

I've closed my eyes
and pretended not to see
weeds growing taller
choking out the fragrant herbs
begging to breathe freely.
Guiltlessly, I've ignored
stacks of compositions
crying out, "Grade us!
End of quarter's almost here!"

I've bristled at my son
and ignored his questions
while selfishly snuggling in bed
with P.D. James's latest mystery.
And stacks of laundry pile up
Phone calls go unanswered
I doze and read undaunted
by life's mundane responsibilities.

—Arlene Swora
(In the style of Lowell Jaeger)

Once I cheated little kids
out of their shiny, new dimes
by saying, "Look at this <u>big</u>
nickel. Wouldn't you <u>love</u> to own
it? It's twice as big as your dime."
It worked every time and
those innocent little kids with
their big lovable eyes made
me the richest 3rd
grader in America.

—Paula Lee

Confession

Sometimes
I choose a mood—
Pick at a remark
Like a scab,
Lifting the edges,
Testing the unhealed center,
Drawing a drop of fresh blood.
No apologies:
A bit of tumult tastes good again
Sometimes.

—Donna-Marie Stupple

What Daddy Doesn't Know

I lied to my father twice.
He was thinking pizza,
while I was partying.
He was better off not knowing.
The second: I was "too young"
for Prom. I went anyway.
He thought dinner, dance, directly home.
I did dinner, dance, scenic lookout, home.

—Amy Besel

Confessions of a Little Kid

Once I had a contest with
myself, to see how many ants
I could crush by stepping on them.
I've thrown my cat off
the stairs to see if he would
really land on his feet.
And, once I caught a toad and
accidentally lost it in my room—
As far as mom knew he was outside,
until, of course, she found him.

—Belle Vukovich

Confession

In the fourth grade I peeked
at Tommy Turner's world geography map,
certain that Miss Annie saw
through her thumb-smudged glasses.
I pretended to be sick,
cried on the cold concrete steps
outside the oiled oak doors of Elementary
where my mother abandoned me on winter mornings.

And then there was the gift
delivered accidentally to my door,
glazed white paper tied in blue satin
hiding in the closet unopened,
glaring like the golden retriever's eyes
who unseeing balked at the steep stairwell
abyss of uncarpeted skids and stops.
I had to drag her down.

—Gerry Jones

Interlude

Confessing, Boasting, or Just Biographying

Any kind of recital can become a poem, listing items that relate to each other, doing an account chapter by chapter or event by event. And if the "I" of the poem tells mostly bits that reveal weaknesses or other flaws, the tone is that of confession. But some kinds of confessing turn into boasting, it seems. In a poem, that's OK.

And such a recital can become an easy-forward recital that takes on momentum as the character of the teller gets more and more revealed by the materials included: every item on the list adds to the realization about the main character. There is no absolutely insignificant element, for all elements are filtered through a person.

There is relief in confession, for the self who is spreading out the past for a calm look; and maybe there are lessons for others too, for their insight and reform.

Monologue Poems

Introduction

Robert Browning's "My Last Duchess" was written more than one hundred years ago. The scene of the poem goes back centuries further to the Italian Renaissance. It may be the most famous monologue poem ever.

(If you *haven't* read it, do so now. It's at the end of this exercise as Text 53. In fact, read it aloud. Then read it aloud *to* someone. It will begin to make eerie sense as you hear it—the Duke talking to an emissary [go-between, agent] from a Count who has a daughter available for marriage. But what happened to the Duke's *last* Duchess? The Duke says he "gave commands." What commands? Read the poem, think about it, talk about it. Please notice the form—five-beat rhyming couplets; then notice how skillfully the lines are arranged so the rhymes are sort of buried: they slide by your ears instead of banging on them. **Or take a dare?** *Memorize* "My Last Duchess"—a mere 56 lines—and say it aloud at parties, when wandering in the halls, and on other occasions. Twenty years from now you'll thank us. We both *absolutely* guarantee it.)

But here's just the start of that famous poem: (from) Text 53

My Last Duchess

That's my last Duchess painted on the wall,
Looking as if she were alive. I call
That piece a wonder, now; Fra Pandolf's hands
Worked busily a day, and there she stands.
Will't please you sit and look at her? . . .

Who's the poem's speaker? (That is, what character "tells" it?)
Easy enough, you say. Our old friend "I." And you can tell (from the title and the poem) "I" is the Duke.

Are there other characters in the poem?
Sure, you say. People the Duke is talking *about,* the Duchess and Fra (Brother) Pandolf. He must be the artist who painted her. Also, *right there in the scene,* there's "you": "Will't please *you* sit and look at her?" (We know from later in the poem that "you" is the emissary from the Count who has a daughter he wants to marry off to the Duke.)

Where and when is this poem taking place?

Hard to tell, just from this excerpt. But you've already made good guesses if you've read the entire poem. For now, go with "Italy in the 1500s."

What's going on?

Well, you say, the Duke seems to be pointing to a painting of his Duchess. The Duke invites the emissary ("you") to sit and have a closer look. Or did the Duke *tell* him to do that? In any case, "you" sits, looks, and listens.

(Good answers.) You can see how, in a monologue poem, there can be more than one character and there can be plenty going on. **But only the speaker talks.** Let's look at a complete poem, one that surely has been influenced by "My Last Duchess." You'll see some tricks that bring voices and action into a monologue.

Text 52

My Last Service

(with a nod to Robert Browning)

Good morning, Mr. Custer. May I
suggest, Sir, the buffalo hump
with corn bread?—you see, our hunters
report game scarce ahead. It seems
that herds have been spooked, Sir, all   (5)
throughout this valley. No, not to me, Sir—
this report I overheard while serving the scouts.

This roast?—my mother, Sir, she
brought it in. A humble woman, Cheyenne,
Sir. And in fact she has invited me   (10)
to accompany her on a slight detour
this morning as you ride north. She says
there may be more meat before tonight.
Thank you, Sir. Have a good day.

"My Last Service" imitates "My Last Duchess." Although there's more to feast on in the longer poem, "My Last Service" is a tasty and crafty dish as well. In fact its fourteen lines display many of the longer monologue's tricks.

The entire poem is one speaker's words. But you can sense some action, too. What "action" happens at the start of the poem? (Perhaps the "waitperson" approaches Custer's table, smiles, and speaks. Maybe Custer is reading reports of hostile Indian activity in the area.) What action do you see at the start of stanza two? What action might there be at the end of the poem?

Before we get into the monologue's tricks, let's repeat the questions above.

Who's the poem's speaker?

A waitress/waiter, a Cheyenne Indian speaking. Male or

female? We're not sure. But we notice that once again the speaker's name is "I."

Are there other characters in the poem?

Well, there's Mr. Custer, although he doesn't actually speak. Unless you know little of U.S. history, you know that Custer is General George Custer. Other characters: the Cheyenne hunters, the speaker's mother.

Where and when is this poem taking place?

History tells us of "Custer's Last Stand" near Little Bighorn, Montana. "Buffalo hump" and other words suggest the post–Civil War West.

What's going on?

Plenty. For one thing, we know something about the speaker's feelings. Although "I's" customer is breakfasting on roast and corn bread, "I's" people face hard times. And "I's" people believe their land has been taken from them by whites. The poem "happens" just before Little Bighorn. "[Mother] says / there may be more meat before tonight."

We suspect Custer *won't* "have a good day."

Close reading will lead us to additional richnesses. Some of the "extra" isn't even on the page. The monologue makes us provide it. How?

There are questions from Custer, even though Custer doesn't *actually* ask them in the poem. We ask them for him. Look in the middle of line 6. What question is asked between the words "*valley*" and "*No*"? And by whom? (Right. Custer asks a question like the one you just said he asked.)

There's another question asked between lines 7 and 8. What's the question? Who asks it? (Right, again.)

In addition to inviting us to provide questions, the monologue lets us provide lines of narrative or dialogue. Recall the last line of the poem:

"Thank you, Sir. Have a good day."

What has Custer *said* or *done* that the speaker is thanking him for?

(Whatever you think Custer *said* or *did,* you had to supply it.)

Monologue Poem Steps

Step 1.

As is the scene of General Custer "brunching" before Little Bighorn, there are "*public situations*" that are *potentially* "*dramatic.*" Let these situations come from history or from "fiction." Or even let them be set "in the future." Here are examples; you'll think of others.

"**Public situations**"

(a) Friday, welcoming Robinson Crusoe ashore

(b) Jesus, speaking at the last supper

(c) Natasha, a Russian child, watching the attempted coup of 1991

(d) The first USA woman president, addressing Congress

(e) Pocahantas's father, greeting her after her date with John Smith

(f) Admirers of leaders (e.g., King or Kennedy) at their assassination

(g) Mona Lisa, answering Leonardo's ad for a model

Do you see those as scenes, or little stories? JOT DOWN ONE OR TWO "PUBLIC SITUATIONS" THAT APPEAL TO YOU. Use your own scenes or ones like examples (a) through (g). Items the length of (a) through (g) have enough detail. Notice that we started each example with "the name" of our speaker—Friday, Jesus, *etc.*). Select scenes with "dramatic possibilities."

You'll need a speaker who tells the poem. It will help to have a "listener" in the poem as well. For example, the emissary ("you") in "My Last Duchess," "Mr. Custer" in "My Last Service." Two silent "listeners."

You must imagine scenes in which it's reasonable that the speaker tell his story. (The Count has sent his emissary to the Duke; it's natural that the Duke discuss his earlier wife. Serving breakfast to Custer in "My Last Service," the speaker naturally talks to his customer.)

Step 2.   Now think of situations from your life that have, or have the potential to have, dramatic possibilities. Think about *"personal situations."* By *personal* we only mean something that connects with you. Can you find potential drama in these?

"Personal situations"

(h) My best friend wants me to do something almost illegal

(i) I'm replaying, in my head, how that argument should have gone

(j) I'm at a wedding I have strong feelings about

(k) I'm giving my side of the fight to my dog (cat, gerbil, _____)

(l) I've found out that someone close to me is ill or in trouble

(m) Applying for work, I've been asked what my work habits are

(n) A parent has come home unexpectedly

In just a few words, as in (h) through (n), JOT DOWN ONE OR TWO "PERSONAL SITUATIONS" THAT APPEAL TO YOU. With personal situations, when you write "I" it will stand for you yourself, or for someone much like you yourself.

Do you *want* "a listener" built into the situation? It's up to you. Your monologue *could be* you thinking, or you talking to yourself. No other character required. But often *having someone else "in the scene" works best.* For example, in (h) the sweetheart or friend; in (j) a member of the wedding party. Or take (n). Say "I" is a fifteen-year-old female and assume her mother has just come through the door.

> Momma! Imagine! I thought
> you were coming home late. Let's see.
> You've met Russell, here, and Sam.
> The way we look you probably think—
> What? You said "Not another soul
> sets foot in *your* house." Momma,
> what could I do? Sam rang the bell . . .

And so on. Use situations of ours or make up ones of your own.

Step 3.   Select the one **public** and the one **personal** situation you're most attracted to. Find room to answer these questions for **both:**

WHO'S SPEAKING? AND TO WHOM?
In your **personal** example, "I" is more or less you yourself. Still, you may want to decide what "parts of yourself" and what attitudes "I" is going to reveal. (Don't let it *all* hang out.) In our example ("Momma! Imagine! . . .") the situation is treated lightly. But personal situations can generate a whole range of feelings—joy or gloom, hope or despair, confidence or fear—and any one situation can produce a variety of responses from different viewers. *By how "I" thinks and talks and does* you can create the feeling and tone you want.

In your **public** example, how you characterize your speaker is important. For example, Is Friday glad to see Crusoe?
Does Jesus know something is awry at the last supper?
Is Natasha for or against the plotters? Is she old enough to understand what she's seeing, or does she simply report, letting the reader interpret?

Knowing your speaker's attitudes and personality will pretty much determine how, and with what feeling, the story is told.
What other characters belong in your poem?
Where is the poem taking place? Jot down clues that could indicate place, time, circumstance. . . .
What's going on?
The monologue poem will tell the stories of those situations you've chosen and thought about. But notice that the stories of both "My Last Duchess" and "My Last Service" are more than their "surface" stories. There's much going on "below the surface" of "My Last Service." Reading "My Last Duchess," you felt the tension and the drama of that poem. How proud and cruel the Duke seems. How subtle the tensions between the Duke and the messenger. What's happened to the Duchess? How will things be for the Count's daughter?

Step 4.   Once you have answered the questions for both public and personal situations, *choose the one that seems to have the most drama, the better story.* You already know who's speaking and whether there are other characters in the poem. You know the story and where it's taking place. You know all you need to know to write.

> *What follows will help you turn jottings into a poem.*

Think of your monologue poem as *all the talk (dialogue) in a very short play. The curtain parts. Events are underway. Your character turns to a listener and tells the story*—that is, "says" the poem.

Think of "My Last Service" that way. The curtain parts. Some officers are being served breakfast by Native Americans. One of these, the speaker of the poem, approaches Custer's table . . . "May I suggest, Sir," he begins.

And think of "My Last Duchess" the same way. The curtain opens. We're on the mezzanine of a grand Renaissance palace. Two male characters. One steps forward to pull aside a cloth that reveals a painting of a young woman.

"That's my last Duchess," he begins.

Step 5.   *Write a monologue poem of fifteen or more lines.*

Remember, only one speaker actually speaks in your poem. But other characters can be talked about, can listen and can even react: See how these are "a kind of speech"?

	Don't wag your head at me. . . .
(or)	I can see you don't believe me.
(or)	Oh good! You turn your back.

Step 6.   Try these tricks from "My Last Service" and "My Last Duchess."

(a) Speaker asks someone a direct question <u>not</u> requiring a direct answer
> *Your name is Mona Lisa? You've come*
> *to see about the posing job? . . .*

(b) Speaker addresses someone "in the poem" by name
> *Now Mother, don't say a word . . .*

(c) Speaker answers a question asked "between the lines"
> *Where did I get this key? I found it near. . . .*
> *(or) This key? I found it near. . . .*

(d) Speaker quotes someone "not in the scene"
> *It's like Ms Coffee says, "That's good.*
> *In fact it's great."*

or tells what someone "on stage" thinks
> *Sure. You think I've lost my nerve . . .*

(e) Speaker describes action "off stage"
> *Yesterday in York I saw a man who said*
> *"Go home. There's nothing here . . ."*

It might seem as if a monologue, with but one speaker, would be limiting and dull. Not so. Such tricks as the question not asked (but answered) and the action not shown (but known) give the illusion of numerous voices in a one-voice poem. So do "rhetorical questions" such as those we looked at in the Question/Answer poem exercise. The speaker can both ask and answer them. (There's a rhetorical question in lines 1–3 of "My Last Service" and numerous examples in "My Last Duchess.")

Step 7.   When you have drafted your monologue, read it aloud, preferably *to* Someone. Does the speaker's talk fit the character ("I") you have in mind? Have you tried some of the tricks listed above? Are there "weak" or "fat places" you can fix or cut? Is there a good part that should be expanded?

Revise according to what you've heard and believe.

Then, **in your Notebook:** *copy that revision.* Actually, if you'll work out loud—or "silently aloud"—you'll probably make other changes as you work. Trust your ear.

Text 53   **My Last Duchess**
That's my last Duchess painted on the wall,
Looking as if she were alive. I call
That piece a wonder, now: Fra Pandolf's hands
Worked busily a day, and there she stands.
Will't please you sit and look at her? I said
"Fra Pandolf" by design, for never read
Strangers like you that pictured countenance,
The depth and passion of its earnest glance,
But to myself they turned (since none puts by
The curtain I have drawn for you, but I)
And seemed as they would ask me, if they durst,
How such a glance came there; so, not the first
Are you to turn and ask thus. Sir, 'twas not
Her husband's presence only, called that spot
Of joy into the Duchess' cheek: perhaps
Fra Pandolf chanced to say, "Her mantle laps
Over my lady's wrist too much," or "Paint
Must never hope to reproduce the faint
Half-flush that dies along her throat." Such stuff
Was courtesy, she thought, and cause enough
For calling up that spot of joy. She had
A heart—how shall I say?—too soon made glad,
Too easily impressed; she liked whate'er
She looked on, and her looks went everywhere.
Sir, 'twas all one! My favor at her breast,
The dropping of the daylight in the West,
The bough of cherries some officious fool
Broke in the orchard for her, the white mule

She rode round the terrace—all and each
Would draw from her alike the approving speech,
Or blush, at least. She thanked men,—good! but thanked
Somehow—I know not how—as if she ranked
My gift of a nine-hundred-years-old name
With anybody's gift. Who'd stoop to blame
This sort of trifling? Even had you skill
In speech—which I have not—to make your will
Quite clear to such an one, and say, "Just this
Or that in you disgusts me; here you miss,
Or there exceed the mark"—and if she let
Herself be lessoned so, nor plainly set
Her wits to yours, forsooth, and made excuse
—E'en then would be some stooping; and I choose
Never to stoop. Oh, sir, she smiled, no doubt
Whene'er I passed her; but who passed without
Much the same smile? This grew; I gave commands;
Then all smiles stopped together. There she stands
As if alive. Will't please you rise? We'll meet
The company below, then. I repeat
The Count your master's known munificence
Is ample warrant that no just pretense
Of mine for dowry will be disallowed;
Though his fair daughter's self, as I avowed
At starting, is my object. Nay, we'll go
Together down, sir. Notice Neptune, though
Taming a sea-horse, thought a rarity,
Which Claus of Innsbruck cast in bronze for me!

—Robert Browning

Poems in Response

Dream

I have to tell you about my dream.
I was walking through a forest,
But it was dark, and there was a thick fog.
I could barely make out the trees.
Then I saw you—Are you listening to me?—
You were standing on the crest of a hill
In the middle of a clearing.
The wisps of the fog seemed to drift away from you,
Allowing the moonbeams to—What are you looking at?
Would you pay attention—filter down,
And surround you in a silver liquid-like light.
   I called your name,
But my voice became lost in the darkness.
   You turned away,
And fog rushed in and swallowed you up.
What do you think that means?

                       —Elizabeth Freimuth

Put your old "Ralph Waldo" here, OK?
I can use your pond, can't I? Just a short lease.

Well . . .
Spend a little time at Walden.
Maybe build a cabin, grow some beans, write a little,
  kinda sort things out, I guess.

A whim? Nah—
Impulsive? No way—
Just some space, a place to slow life,
To put the glass right up against it, to front life
And track it. Every bit of it.

Out of touch?
More in touch than ever. In touch for everyone. To catch
Each ant and fish and bean
Alive, all life,
All god.
Every bit of it.

                       —Kathy Cardille

That Secret Look

Leonardo, shhh, come here,
See the strange woman
With the secret look,
Sitting there waiting
So expectantly?

Notice those eyes.

Can you imagine this
Plain-looking woman
Actually answering
your ad for a model?
You, the great . . .

Oh! Observe her lips' slight curve.

What a strange smile!
Will wonders never cease?
Imagine the nerve of such
A curious, mousey creature's
coming here to you, Leonardo.

What? Oh, her name?
Well, it's funny, too,
Something like Mona . . .
Ummm, yes, Mona,
      Mona Lisa.

What, Send her in, you say?
Wellll, well yes, of course.
I'll call her at once, Sir.

Mona Lisa, please
step this way.

                         —Jean Copland

THE TRIAL

Oh, sir . . . I mean "sirs";
it happened too fast.
The night was closing in,
my brain cloudy—yes, I'd been drinking.
The median strips were blurring,
either colliding or spreading all over the road.
And there she was, sirs,
all of a sudden.
A blur of white, a flash of metal,

and she was under my car,
helpless and dead.
See her mother crying?
See her hide behind a soaked tissue?
And you, your Honor, seem aghast that
I recall it so well and unashamedly.
What's that?
Restrain myself, dear sirs?
I'm sorry,
but after that first drink
there is no restraining . . .

and I took that drink long ago.

—Lena James

Daddy, Can We Talk

Daddy, I'm home.
I know, I know, don't
be mad though, the car
broke down.

Yes, I did have fun.
No, I'm fine. Well first
we went to see a movie
then we went for a
drive. Don't look at me
that way, he was a
perfect gentleman.

Why do I look so pre-
occupied? I just have
things on my mind.
He asked me to marry
him Daddy.

Of course I love him.
I don't know if I
want to get married
yet. What should I
do?

Okay, I know. I'll make
my own decision.

—Tracy Valstad

Interlude

Letting the Voice Take Over

A voice always has a context, a setting, some implications of before and after, some tone that hints at the real speaker, and then the *persona* or mask assumed by the speaker for this one utterance.

If only the one speaker is there, how do these other elements, and the drama of the scene, get conveyed?

To ask such a question is like opening a whole new book; for where the voice begins its message, how long it stays on each part of the message, what words are chosen, how the whole is paced or punctuated or broken into lines, even what kind of ink or type is used—everything makes a difference.

You can manage it all. By hints in the wording you can make a reader know the setting, something of the events earlier, and plenty about the speaker and the persons spoken to. You the writer make the choices. And you can't hide, either. The result of your writing is a picture of you.

Imitation 4

Imitation Steps

Step 1.

Find a poem you really like.

Here, with our blessings, are four poems *we* admire. But feel free to search out and use a poem you prefer. (We're going to ask you do a "general imitation," so find a poem *you* truly admire.)

Text 54

Summons

Keep me from going to sleep too soon
Or if I go to sleep too soon
Come wake me up. Come any hour
Of night. Come whistling up the road.
Stomp on the porch. Bang on the door.
Make me get out of bed and come
And let you in and light a light.
Tell me the northern lights are on
And make me look. Or tell me clouds
Are doing something to the moon
They never did before, and show me.
See that I see. Talk to me till
I'm half as wide awake as you
And start to dress wondering why
I ever went to bed at all.
Tell me the walking is superb.
Not only tell me but persuade me.
You know I'm not too hard persuaded.

—Robert Francis

Text 55

Mirror

I am silver and exact. I have no preconceptions.
Whatever I see I swallow immediately
Just as it is, unmisted by love or dislike.
I am not cruel, only truthful—
The eye of a little god, four-cornered.
Most of the time I meditate on the opposite wall.
It is pink, with speckles. I have looked at it so long
I think it is a part of my heart. But it flickers.
Faces and darkness separate us over and over.

Now I am a lake. A woman bends over me,
Searching my reaches for what she really is.
Then she turns to those liars, the candles or the moon.

I see her back, and reflect it faithfully.
She rewards me with tears and an agitation of hands.
I am important to her. She comes and goes.
Each morning it is her face that replaces the darkness.
In me she has drowned a young girl, and in me an old woman
Rises toward her day after day, like a terrible fish.

—Sylvia Plath

Text 56

Eating Poetry

Ink runs from the corners of my mouth,
There is no happiness like mine.
I have been eating poetry.

The librarian does not believe what she sees.
Her eyes are sad
and she walks with her hands in her dress.

The poems are gone.
The light is dim.
The dogs are on the basement stairs and coming up.

Their eyebrows roll,
their blonde legs burn like brush.
The poor librarian begins to stamp her feet and weep.

She does not understand.
When I get on my knees and lick her hand,
she screams.

I am a new man.
I snarl at her and bark.
I romp with joy in the bookish dark.

—Mark Strand

Text 57

The Traveling Onion

It is believed that the onion originally came
from India. In Egypt it was an object of worship
—why I haven't been able to find out. From
Egypt the onion entered Greece and on to Italy,
thence into all of Europe.

Better Living Cookbook

When I think how far the onion has traveled
just to enter my stew today, I could kneel and praise
all small forgotten miracles,
crackly paper peeling on the drainboard,
pearly layers in smooth agreement,
the way knife enters onion
and onion falls apart on the chopping block,
a history revealed.

And I would never scold the onion
for causing tears.
It is right that tears fall

for something small and forgotten.
How at meal, we sit to eat,
commenting on texture of meat or herbal aroma
but never on the translucence of onion,
now limp, now divided,
or its traditionally honorable career:
For the sake of others,
disappear.

—Naomi Shihab Nye

Step 2. Make an exact *hand-written* copy of the poem you've chosen. As you copy, sound the poem in your head. (That is, read it "silently aloud.")

Check your copy against the original. One good way is to have someone else read silently from your copy as you read the original aloud—giving spellings, punctuations, line-breaks, etc. Be sure to put the poet's name on your copy.

Step 3. Now work with your copy. Pen (or highlighter) in hand, again read the poem aloud and note specific things you admire and can imitate. Here's a partial list of possibilities:

- beginnings—"in medias res"—scene, personae, action "under way"
- repetitions of language and/or sounds
- strong, vivid, exact images
- comparisons, especially similes and metaphors
- places where the poem sounds especially musical or rhythmically interesting
- "moves" or "turns," catapulting the poem forward
- patterns of images; echoes of images and sounds
- line breaks that create surprises, interest you

When you've read closely and noted things you admire, specify three or four "characteristics" you're going to try for in your imitation.

Step 4. Still working with your copy of the model poem, *copy-change at least three beginnings from the model. Imitate the way the model poem gets under way.* Avoid the exact subject of the model poem.

For example, in "Summons" you might imitate the way "the speaker" gives directions to some unnamed "you." But transform the subject (the speaker's directives to be awakened, so as not to miss anything) to something of your own—to something **serious** ("Give me a hand up this hill . . ." or "Help me not tumble into love . . .") or something **light** ("Keep me from eating too much . . ." or "Say how algebra works . . .").

From "Mirror" you might adopt an object as your speaker ("I").

See how in "Eating Poetry" the speaker ("I") becomes dog-like and eats something (poetry) that is normally read.

"The Travelling Onion" begins with an *epigraph*, a quotation from a cookbook, using it as the occasion for a poem.

Work from the poem you like best, borrowing from the model words and techniques that will help you get underway and keep things moving. (Don't ignore those little structure-setting words—then, since, or, now, after, when, under, while . . .)

Step 5. Look over your marked-up copy of the model poem. Then read your three copy-changed beginnings. Select the one that seems most promising, or the one that seems the best imitation, and develop it fully. Keep one eye on your exact copy as you work, going to the text when you want or need to, leaving the original text behind when your own poem is moving well.

Step 6. When you're content with your imitation (or when you're willing to "abandon it," as someone has said), stop work and credit the model—whether or not there are exact correspondences of language and style.

If the imitation is close to the original, use as credit such as "In the manner of 'Summons,' by Robert Francis." If the model poem has more or less disappeared from your imitation, use a more general credit, such as "After reading Sylvia Plath's 'Mirror.'"

Postlude

Coming Up for Air

Those authors of books, those models we just used, like Sylvia Plath, Robert Francis, and the others, did they ever wonder about what to do with their writings? Did they have any duds on their hands? What do you think?

If you have written your way through this book, you have yourself accumulated a book, one with variety, depth, and much revelation about the person involved in the writing.

You can share with friends, if you find that something you have written might appeal to and relate to someone you know. And as for wider circulation, that depends on your sense of how what you have written might help others.

Think of editors as people who need material. If you have something that would help them, you could mail it off with a brief note telling why you think your enclosure might be of value. How accurate you are in your estimate depends on your acquaintance with the needs of the editor—and that takes some reading and thinking on your part. No need to batter against the editor's door with something you can't conceive of as helpful.

Much of what anyone writes will be less than ideal for someone else's purposes, but be generous if you have something worthy to put under the attention of a reader. We're in this together. And every one of us is unique, with something for someone somewhere.

Listen. We've enjoyed our work on this book. Have you? During our writing, we heard from dozens of students and teachers. The poems and messages they sent us were both interesting and fresh. We hope our book reflects those readers.

Now to old friends and new, it's time to say, "Enjoy your work. Good luck with the writing. Adios."

Credits

Text 1, "Wanted by Sheriff," by William Stafford.

Text 2, "Prairie Wind," by Stephen Dunning.

Text 3, "Workaday Worm," by Stephen Dunning.

Text 4, "Bad News," by William Stafford.

Text 5, "Dear Art Herring," by Stephen Dunning.

Text 6, "Dear William Stafford," by William Stafford, originally published as "Dear Sir," in a series of broadsides by Wang Hui Ming.

Text 7, "Dear Husband," by Dorothy Schieber Miller and Stephen Dunning. Used with permission of the authors.

Text 8, "Recipe for School-type Chicken Soup," by Stephen Dunning, first appeared in a slightly different form in *Holidays & Celebrations*, 1984.

Text 9, Excerpted from "Building a Person," by Stephen Dunn. Reprinted from Stephen Dunn: *A Circus of Needs* by permission of Carnegie Mellon University Press © 1978 by Stephen Dunn.

Text 10, "The Grocer's Children," by Herbert Scott. Reprinted from *Groceries,* by Herbert Scott, by permission of the University of Pittsburgh Press. © 1976 by Herbert Scott.

Text 11, "Cache Street North," by William Stafford, was originally published as "Gutters of Jackson: Cache Street North," in *Smoke's Way,* Graywolf Press, 1983.

Text 12, "The third baseman dreams . . ." by Stephen Dunning, is excerpted from "Baseball Player List," first published in *New Virginia Review,* 1979.

Text 13, "Big Jim Dunks One Through," by Stephen Dunning and Andrew Carrigan. An earlier version of this poem, entitled "Big Lew Dunks One Through," appeared in *Poetry: Voices, Language, Forms,* published by Scholastic in 1970.

Text 14, "The Summer We Didn't Die," by William Stafford, originally published in *Passwords,* by HarperCollins in 1991.

Text 15, "Heckedy Peg," by Martha Demerly; used with the author's permission.

Text 16, "Cold," by William Stafford.

Text 17, "These two . . ." by Stephen Dunning.

Text 18, "There are . . . " by Stephen Dunning.

Text 42, "Two Friends," by David Ignatow, was published in *Figures of the Human*. "Two Friends" © 1964, by David Ignatow.

Text 43, "Shopping," by Dorothy Schieber Miller. Used with permission of the author.

Text 44, "Plus," by Raymond Carver. Copyright © by Tess Gallagher. Reprinted by permission of Tess Gallagher.

Text 45, "Forgive," by Stephen Dunning.

Text 46, "Ode on a Big Leg Woman," by Jeff Stockton. Used with permission of the author.

Text 47, "Fear," by Raymond Carver. Copyright © by Tess Gallagher. Reprinted by permission of Tess Gallagher.

Text 48, "Painting the Gate," by May Swenson. © 1976 by May Swenson and used with the permission of the literary estate of May Swenson.

Text 49, "Dreams," by Langston Hughes, is from *The Dream Keeper and Other Poems*, by Langston Hughes. © 1932 by Alfred A. Knopf, Inc. and renewed 1960 by Langston Hughes. Reprinted by permission of the publisher.

Text 50, "My Self," by Stephen Dunning, was first published in *Concerning Poetry*, 1977.

Text 51, Excerpted from "Confessions," by Lowell Jaeger. Reprinted with permission of the author.

Text 52, "My Last Service," by William Stafford, was originally published in *Michigan Quarterly Review*.

Text 53, "My Last Duchess," by Robert Browning.

Text 54, "Summons," by Robert Francis, is reprinted from *Robert Francis: Collected Poems, 1936-1976*. Amherst: University of Massachusetts Press, 1976. © 1944, 1972 by Robert Francis. Used with permission.

Text 55, "Mirror," by Sylvia Plath. From *The Collected Poems of Sylvia Plath*, edited by Ted Hughes. Copyright © 1963 by Ted Hughes. Reprinted by permission of HarperCollins Publishers.

Text 56, "Eating Poetry," by Mark Strand. Used with the author's permission.

Text 57, "The Traveling Onion," by Naomi Shihab Nye, is reprinted by permission of the author, NSN.

Authors

Photo credit: Kit Stafford

Photo credit: Mel Manis

William Stafford has taught high school and college, worked in the fields, in construction, for an oil refinery, for the U.S. Forest Service, for Church World Service, as Poetry Consultant for the Library of Congress. . . . The first of his eight collections with Harper & Row, *Traveling Through the Dark*, won the National Book Award. Two of his books on writing and the writing life are *You Must Revise Your Life* and *Writing the Australian Crawl*, from the University of Michigan Press. Publications in 1992 include a collection, *My Name is William Tell*, and (with artist Debra Fraser) a children's book, *The Animal That Drank Up Sound*. He has lectured widely for the U.S. Information Service in Egypt, India, Pakistan, Iran, Nepal, Bangladesh, Singapore, and Thailand.

Stephen Dunning taught high school English in St. Paul, Los Alamos, and Tallahassee before teaching English education at Duke, Northwestern, and The University of Michigan. His earliest publications were articles, texts, and (as co-editor with Lueders and Smith) such anthologies as *"Reflection On A Gift Of Watermelon Pickle . . ."* In 1975, the year he served as President of NCTE, he began writing poetry and, in 1984, fiction. His poems are gathered in six chapbooks—one, *Running With Bill* (1985), is dedicated to Stafford. His collection of short fiction is *To The Beautiful Women* (1990). Recognitions include winning the "Tamarack Award," the "World's Best Short Short Story" contest, the "James B. Hall Award for Short Fiction," two creative artist grants, and five PEN Syndicated Fiction awards.

Stafford and Dunning met at the NCTE Convention in Houston in 1966. They became friends and subsequently survived collaboration. Both practice regularly as writers; both give readings and workshops, judge contests, and teach short courses around the country.